POST-MODERN

MODERN

BUILDINGS IN BRITAIN

POST-MODERN

BUILDINGS IN BRITAIN

Geraint Franklin and Elain Harwood

BATSFORD

Contents

Origins

By the 1970s there was a widespread sense of a crisis in modernism. The high-tech of Richard Rogers and Norman Foster, new materials such as plastics and principles of sustainable architecture all offered a way out. The decade also witnessed a revived use of brick that led to explorations into neo-vernacular, Arts and Crafts traditions, classicism and conservation. Out of this disorder one trend weaved elements of old and new, not into a consistent idiom but into an eclectic architecture that was, at its best, individual and adventurous.

Post-modernism in architecture is characterized by its plurality, engagement with urban context and setting, reference to older architectural traditions and use of metaphors and symbols to suggest several ideas at once. Its unexpected exaggerations and distortions of conventional proportions suggest links to the mannerism of the late Renaissance, while unusual delineations of space have been likened to the 17th-century Baroque style. These traits were beginning to appear by 1977 when Charles Jencks, an American critic and historian based in London, published *The Language of Post-Modern Architecture*.

Post-modern architecture can be defined by its relationship with modernism. On one level it was a reaction to the excesses and broken promises of the modernist establishment. Charles Jencks claimed the dynamiting of part of the Pruitt–Igoe housing project in St Louis, Missouri, in 1972 as the death of modern architecture. But in truth, each post-modernist had their own Pruitt–Igoe moment. Reactions varied; some reformed and enriched modernism from within, widening its scope through historical or regional connections. Others felt that the original aspirations of modernism could only be realized through alternative strategies.

Like all stylistic labels the term 'post-modernism' is overused, but it has more value than most, with the supreme advantage of being contemporary rather than retrospectively applied by historians. Outside architecture, it relates to movements in other arts, literature and philosophy. The term is an old one, used in painting in the 1880s, literature from the 1930s and popular fiction from the early 1960s.[1] Joseph Hudnut applied it to buildings in 1949 in his 1945 article on 'The Post-Modern House'[2], a criticism of the mechanized architecture he had taught at the Bauhaus.[3] Nikolaus Pevsner called 'post-modern' the architecture he considered 'the legitimate style of the nineteen-fifties and nineteen-sixties' – the refined modernism of architects such as Arne Jacobsen or Powell and Moya – when in 1966 he attacked the brutalists or 'anti-pioneers'.[4]

From 1975 the strands were brought together by Charles Jencks, a figure who has become more closely identified with post-modernism in architecture than any other, and who defined it in terms of a 'double-coded language – one part modern and one part something else'.[6] C Ray Smith had used the alternative 'supermannerism' in a series of late-1960s articles gathered into a 1977 book of that name.[7] In the early work of Robert Venturi and especially Charles Moore, Smith identified the layering or separation of elements, the use of cut-out shapes and over-scaled lettering – termed 'supergraphics' – and references to aspects of mass culture, such as comic books. In 1977, the architect Robert A M Stern used the term in the manner that has become universal:

> Post-modernism recognizes that buildings are designed to mean something, that they are not hermetically sealed objects. Post-modernism accepts diversity; it prefers hybrids to pure forms; it encourages multiple and simultaneous readings in its effort to heighten expressive content. Borrowing from forms and strategies of both modernism and the architecture that preceded it, post-modernism declares the pastness of both. The layering of space characteristic of much post-modernist architecture finds its complement in the overlay of cultural and art-historical references in the elevations. For the post-modernist, 'more is more'. [5]

The most distinctive strand of post-modern architecture originated in the United States. Louis Kahn provides an important bridge between modernists and post-modernists in offering a common source of inspiration, and his emphasis on separating the service areas that supported the functioning of a building greatly informed Richard Rogers and the high-tech movement. In the 1960s Kahn adopted increasingly bold geometric shapes and a monumentality that fused modern and ancient traditions. His teaching assistant at the University of Philadelphia, Robert Venturi, flattened and stacked these geometries, introducing diagonal movement into the plan, as Kahn had done. The latter's Esherick House in Chestnut Hill, Philadelphia

Vanna Venturi House, designed by Robert Venturi for his mother from 1959, built 1962–4

(1961) exudes the universal qualities of strength and formality whereas, at the end of the same street, Venturi's house designed for his mother (the Vanna Venturi house, 1959–64) offers a series of layered skins, with symmetrical elements countered by informalities and idiosyncrasies and its show front split open to reveal a monumental chimney, a take on a settlers' vernacular.

Two years later, in 1966, Venturi published *Complexity and Contradiction in Architecture*, a study of architecture that focused heavily on the Baroque era but which also embraced Alvar Aalto and Edwin Lutyens. A paperback second edition appeared in 1977. He suggested how 'an artful discord gives vitality to architecture' and a richer experience in urban design. The sources of stateside post-modernism ranged from the colonial classicism and flat, boarded Shingle style of the New England school of architects to the Bauhaus, Art Deco and Pop Art. Yet although modernism and post-modernism shared connections with Kahn, Gunnar Asplund and the Italian rationalists of the 1930s, battle lines soon developed within the American avant-garde, for example between the 'white' post-Corbusians (led by Peter Eisenman) and the 'grays' (Romaldo Giurgola, Allan Greenberg, Charles Moore, Jaquelin T Robertson and Robert Stern) whose one-off private houses were – like Venturi's – less pristine as images but suggested a greater richness and ambiguity in their symbols and layered historical references.

When Denise Scott Brown took a teaching job in Los Angeles she invited her future husband, Robert Venturi, to join her in a research programme in Las Vegas. Venturi had already written on the value of 'honky-tonk elements in the landscape' but his, Denise Scott Brown and Steven Izenour's *Learning from Las Vegas*, published in 1972, further challenged the boundaries between the high art of the academy and the low art of small-town America. Venturi's *Complexity and Contradiction* had criticized the ideas of another Louis Kahn follower, Peter Blake, whose *God's Own Junkyard* in 1964 had derided the kitsch of Long Island's Big Duck, a farmer's market of 1930 in the form of a giant, walk-in duck.[8] The collaborators contrasted the duck building, which for them suggested the modernist integration of structure, space and programme into a single, symbolic object, with the ubiquitous clapboard shed signified only by an applied façade or a roadside sign.

Venturi, Scott Brown and Izenour's acceptance of the ordinary and the everyday found parallels in the recognition of older buildings and thence the retention of characterful but unexceptional stretches of traditional Main Street. Jane Jacobs had argued against their wholesale replacement, asserting that town centres needed buildings of different ages and rents if they were to have a visual and economic diversity, her book *The Death and Life of Great American Cities* in 1961 marking the beginnings of the conservation movement. Stuart Cohen and Colin Rowe described architecture and urban design as a collage of shapes and ideas, and in 'Collage City', an article that led in 1978 to an eponymous book with Fred Koetter, the English-born Rowe argued for urban design based on fragmentation, 'bricolage' and a variety of meanings to secure this diversity.

Charles Moore was another former teaching assistant to Louis Kahn, and his 1961 house in Orinda, California shares references to temples and Roman domestic architecture with Kahn's bath house at Trenton, New Jersey. After becoming Dean of the Yale School of Architecture, Moore transformed a small 19th-century house in 1966–7 with light shafts, over-scaled geometrical cut-outs, bright colours and supergraphics. The same elements brought irony to the collegiate setting of the Faculty Club at the University of California, Santa Barbara of 1967–8. Moore's idea of an inclusive and diverse architecture manifested itself in a public square celebrating New Orleans's small Italian community, the Piazza d'Italia of 1975–9. He placed colonnades and a bell tower resembling theatrical sets around a fountain designed as a three-dimensional map of Italy, their capitals serving as uplighters and trimmed in neon, while water spurted from medallions modelled on Moore's own face.

In Italy, architects championed a different form of post-modernism, seeking not to add to modernism but to strip classicism back to its essence, without the obsession for details found among traditionalists. For Paolo Portoghesi, post-modernism was about the re-emergence of archetypes and conventions, a means of communication or 'civilisation of the image'.[9] He combined an architectural practice based in Rome with a study of architectural history, in particular the work of Francesco Borromini, a leading figure in the emergence of the Baroque architectural style. Portoghesi's own work combined historic references and flowing space, as in his mosque and Islamic centre in Rome of 1975-6, light and uplifting if very Western in its inspiration. In Milan, Ernesto Rogers had referenced early Gothic symbols in his Torre Velasca as early as 1958.

Rogers's pupil Aldo Rossi argued that the historical city offered a vocabulary of types along with a grammar for their combination. Published at a time of unprecedented urban reconstruction, his 1966 book *Architettura della Città* suggested that modern architecture might learn from the collective and communal values of the city, the continuity of its fabric and its compound of anonymity and monumentality. In 1971, while recovering from serious injury after a car crash, Rossi designed an extension to the San Cataldo Cemetery at Modena, an enigmatic assembly of forms dominated by a cubic, ochre-rendered ossuary. This roofless house of the dead offers a poetic metaphor for Rossi's description of the city as a repository of collective memory.

Rossi, Massimo Scolari and others organized the international architecture exhibition at the Milan Triennale in 1973, later published as *Architettura Razionale*. Others associated with the movement termed *La Tendenza* or, more often, neo-rationalism included Carlo Aymonino, Giorgio Grassi and Vittorio Gregotti in Italy; Josef Paul Kleihues and Oswald Mathias Ungers in Germany, and Bruno Reichlin and Fabio Reinhardt in Switzerland. Léon Krier, Maurice Culot and Demetri Porphyrios pursued a form of neo-rationalism more closely allied to a revival of the classical orders. In 1975 Krier organized his own 'Rational Architecture' exhibition at the Art Net gallery in London as a corrective to Rossi's; it featured his own schemes alongside works by Scolari, Grassi, Ungers and his former employer, James Stirling. In the Italian-speaking Ticino canton of Switzerland, a fast-growing economy and a local school of architecture generated a distinctive architecture that combined stark volumes of brick and stone with classical references. At Mario Botta's Bianchi House at Riva San Vitale (1972–3), the Danilo House at Ligornetto (1975–6) and the Medici House at Stabio (1980–2) voids are carved out of solid cubes and cylinders. In later and larger works an affinity with the brick geometries of Louis Kahn is even more apparent.

The Austrian architect Hans Hollein provides a link between Europe and America, having studied, and later taught, in the United States. His early works, such as the Retti candle shop (1965), the Schullin I jewellery store (1974) and two offices of the Austrian Travel Agency (1978) – all in Vienna – and the Abguineh Museum in Tehran, Iran (1978) combined irony, symbolism and a sensuous materiality. In furniture and industrial design other Italian designers pursued bold, gestural shapes, as with the work of Ettore Sottsass and Alessandro Mendini, while Aldo Rossi, Michael Graves,

Addition to the San Cataldo Cemetery by Aldo Rossi, designed 1971, 1976; built 1978–85 (uncompleted)

House for Liliana and Ovidio Medici (Casa Rotunda), Stabio, Switzerland, by Mario Botta, 1980–2

Hollein and others produced designs for Alessi and Sottsass's company, Memphis. Exaggerations of scale were also a feature of post-modernism in Japan, where cubic grids and divergent materials and colours were superimposed on to brutalist concrete forms, a tradition well established in the country after many of its leading architects had worked for Le Corbusier.

The twin traditions of post-modernism contrast in the emphasis they placed on ornament and image, both big in the United States, versus the inheritance of the city, which was particularly important in Europe. Britain, as in many aspects of life and culture, combined elements from both continents when its own post-modernism took shape in the later 1970s. The North American influences proved easiest to understand and absorb, whereas the European stream was more illusive and its urban aspirations were frustrated by first being confined to projects. The two cultures were bridged by the brain drain of British and continental architects invited to teach at East Coast universities – such as Colin Rowe, who taught at Cornell University from 1962 to 1990 – and by Peter Eisenman's Institute for Architecture and Urban Studies in Manhattan, New York, which provided connections to European theory and philosophy and published an influential journal, *Oppositions*.

14

The international factions of post-modernism converged at the first international architectural Biennale held in Venice in 1980. A committee led by Paolo Portoghesi invited architects from around the world to contribute to a display themed as 'The Presence of the Past'. An accompanying catalogue set out four different aspects of the movement; a fifth aspect that was critical of the genre was not submitted, its author, Kenneth Frampton, having withdrawn from the organizing committee. Portoghesi laid out the Arsenale's historic rope works as the Strada Novissima, a concourse in which 20 architects (none of whom were British) designed façades that demonstrated the richness and variety of new ideas emerging under the general heading of post-modernism. The works of British architects Jeremy Dixon, Terry Farrell, Michael Gold, Edward Jones and Quinlan Terry featured in the upstairs gallery. The Strada Novissima followed the success of another three-dimensional exhibit, when in November 1979 Aldo Rossi had floated a temporary theatre on a barge, *Il Teatro del Mondo* (The Theatre of the World), around the Venice archipelago. While a viewing platform offered storey-high views of Venice, the theatre's childlike form, at once classical and yet somehow otherworldly, made a striking impact on the familiar Venice skyline.

The British journal *Architectural Design* held its own exhibition in 1981, choosing Jeremy Dixon, Terry Farrell, Piers Gough, James Gowan, Edward Jones and John Outram to exhibit alongside drawings by Robert Stern. These architects plus James Stirling, then building abroad, formed the backbone of post-modernism in Britain, bolstered by the theory and polemics of Charles Jencks. An accompanying debate focused on the value of post-modern classicism as a universal language for the urban landscape, in which Jeremy Dixon questioned the labels post-modern, rationalist, neoclassicist and neo-vernacular, all of which had been applied to his housing in Kensington.[10] Only Gough and his practice, Campbell Zogolovitch Wilkinson and Gough (CZWG), have unreservedly accepted the post-modernist label.

Meanwhile, British architects sustained themselves through the recession of the early 1980s with exhibition work and temporary buildings. Gough transformed London's Hayward Gallery into a series of settings for the work of Edwin Lutyens and Gertrude Jekyll, while Gowan produced a bright yellow bookshop for the Royal College of Art for a three-week exhibition in 1985, replete with portholes and flaming capitals. Buildings intended to be temporary offered the greatest opportunity for experimentation, seen in 1980 when Farrell designed two flower shops for Clifton Nurseries. The first was a curvaceous steel shed with a cut-out front, erected close to Paddington Station. The second, in Covent Garden, had Tuscan columns that directly faced those of St Paul's Church, just across the piazza – this building lasted from 1981 to 1988, before being re-erected at the Waterways Garden Centre in Clwyd, North Wales.

The Architectural Association (AA) in London was a melting pot of ideas. Alvin Boyarsky, Chairman from 1971 to 1990 and a consummate networker, organized the teaching as a series of diverse units deliberately designed to challenge each other, with an international focus reflected in the origins and approaches of tutors and unit masters. They included Charles Jencks, who had taught there since 1968, Léon Krier, Daniel Libeskind, Bernard Tschumi and Elia Zhenghelis. The AA tradition of having key graduates stay on and teach continued with Rem Koolhaas, who joined the staff in 1975, followed in 1978 by his own former student, Zaha Hadid. Tschumi's student Nigel Coates started teaching in 1977. Staff debates continued at Art Net, the public gallery run between 1973 and 1978 by AA teacher and Archigram designer Peter Cook.

The growth of British post-modernism coincided with upheavals in architectural publishing. *Architectural Design* had been the most dynamic British magazine since the mid-1950s, but had long been in financial difficulties. It was bought in 1975 by the publisher Andreas Papadakis, who repackaged it from 1978 as a sequence of book-length double issues. Many were based around post-modernism and edited by Charles Jencks, for whom Papadakis also published *The Language of Post-Modern Architecture* through multiple editions, amongst other titles. As Britain's leading magazine, the *Architectural Review* became increasingly international; the *Architects' Journal* took over as the leading mouthpiece for British buildings and related subjects of interest. The more discursive, critical writing in the latter was supported by advances in cheap printing, particularly of high-quality colour photographs by Martin Charles, Richard Bryant and Peter Cook. *Architecture Today*, launched in 1989, was also solidly architectural. In 1983 Peter Murray and Deyan Sudjic began *Blueprint* to integrate architecture and design; while the magazine embraced all styles, the multi-disciplinary approach was particularly suited to post-modernism where the links with furniture and product design represented a whole new consumer-led lifestyle. Such links had long been made in the Italian magazines *Domus* and *Casabella*, the international style guides for the era.

British post-modernism remained more contextual than that of other countries, strong in its references not only to classicism but also to Dutch brick traditions, Art Deco, the English Arts and Crafts Movement and the Vienna Secession. A Charles Rennie Mackintosh revival was sustained by the restoration of several buildings and the incorporation of interiors from No. 78 Southpark Avenue, Glasgow into the Hunterian Museum and Art Gallery extension by William Whitfield, opened in 1981. The most interesting work tends to be the least deferential, much of it planned before London's economic boom in the late 1980s. Most is modest in scale or occupies constrained sites, for – in contrast to the United States and Europe – even the most prestigious projects were generally extensions of older buildings.

Strada Novissima, Venice Biennale, 1980, featuring (from left to right) facades by Josef Paul Kleihues, Hans Hollein, Massimo Scolari and Allan Greenberg

The revival of classical architecture in Britain, in contrast to the post-modern position, was based on an irreconcilable opposition to modernism. The architecture of the late Georgian era, imagined as if the Victorian Gothic Revival had never happened, survived right through the 20th century for some public buildings and country houses, thanks to traditionalists such as Francis Johnson. Classicism enjoyed a revival in the 1970s amid a growing enthusiasm for country houses, architectural history and conservation, supported by the historian David Watkin and the Prince of Wales (not least with the development from 1993 onwards of Poundbury, Dorset, based on Léon Krier's theories of urban planning). They pushed to the fore those architects who treated classicism academically and seriously, such as Quinlan Terry and Robert Adam, both Rome Scholars, whose domestic work closely followed traditional models. Underlying the classical revival was an ambivalent attitude to modernity, exemplified by the breeze block cavity wall construction of much of Poundbury. By contrast, the post-modernists were firmly rooted in modernist backgrounds – as was explained by John Outram, Terry's contemporary at the AA, 'I used to like modernism but wanted to make it usable, unlike the double breasted Doric Brigade'.[11]

The position of Krier and Demetri Porphyrios is more complex. Porphyrios settled in London, where his smaller commissions firmly follow the classical tradition, as do those of Krier, born in Luxembourg and a champion of the elegant, early 19th-century neoarclassicism of Frederick Schinkel. Krier quit his university studies to work for James Stirling, just as the latter was discovering neo-classicism. Having met his future wife and obtained a teaching job at the AA he then settled in Britain for 20 years. Porphyrios has criticized post-modernism and stylistic pluralism as unserious and kitsch; nevertheless his work at **Brindleyplace**, Birmingham, challenges these margins. Krier's architecture – until recently confined to paper – is an imaginative abstraction of urban building types rather than an archaeologically correct classicism.

Charles Jencks set out his evolving architectural worldview to the Royal Institute of British Architects (RIBA) in Hull in 1976, speaking alongside a group of architects he labelled his 'revisionist heroes'.[12] They included Terry Farrell, an architect–planner beginning to explore a variety of styles while working in partnership with the high-tech aficionado Nicholas Grimshaw, and John Darbourne, Robert Maguire and Ralph Erskine – all architects who worked in brick or concrete block, but with pitched roofs; they considered every detail of the brief and site, and met the eventual users face-to-face. While Jencks claimed for post-modernism the integrity, urban grain and brilliant colour of Erskine's Byker development in Newcastle, these architects never questioned their modernist credentials; by the early 1980s they and similarly minded practitioners, such as Peter Aldington and Edward Cullinan, came to be labelled romantic pragmatists for the way their designs evolved in imaginative ways from a client's brief. They produced occasional schools for Hampshire County Council Architect's Department under Colin Stansfield Smith, whose highly regarded building programme was grounded in a respect for setting and the adoption of bold geometric shapes and traditional materials.

Rather closer to post-modernism was the work of Richard MacCormac, who combined vernacular elements with direct classical references in his work at Oxford. Such architects formed the backbone in Britain of 'critical regionalism', a term coined by Alex Tzonis and Liliane Lefaivre in 1981 and most widely promoted by the British-born, American-based critic Kenneth Frampton.[13] A more distinctive admixture of sources was provided by an earlier generation, when in the late 1940s Herbert Tayler and David Green took the long terraces they had seen in Ernst May's Frankfurt suburbs and applied tiled roofs, brick patterns, trellises and undulating crinkle-crankle walls from local vernacular sources. The confection led Pevsner again to use the term 'post-modern' in 1962, coming closer this time to its eventual meaning. By 1980 a vernacular revival was spreading across southern England, led by Essex County Council's *Design Guide for Residential Areas*, published in 1973 and becoming a developers' style manual of pitched roofs, brick and weatherboarding. It was very easy to add classical porches or Art Deco porthole windows, as seen at Essex County Council's new town, South Woodham Ferrers, where the supermarket took the form of a giant traditional barn with a clock tower, the first of the genre.

South Woodham Ferrers typified a new form of public sector initiative that was delivered by private developers. In 1981 RIBA finally eased its restrictions on qualified architects acting as developers, though technically they could not be both on the same site. This change encouraged innovative small housing and office schemes, mostly in up-and-coming parts of London. For Terry Farrell the private sector offered more radical options than seemed possible under a flagging welfare state. London's derelict warehouses and gap sites provided opportunities for building new live/work environments, in addition to the shops and bars with which young architects traditionally cut their teeth. The opportunities were seized upon by a generation of architects who came of age in the counter-cultural 1960s, influenced by Rachel Carson's *Silent Spring* (1962) and Jacobs as much as the disposable pop culture of Archigram and Cedric Price. For them, working with small-scale entrepreneurs or community groups represented freedom rather than compromise.

Many felt that the permissive and critical aspects of post-modernism were betrayed in the mid-1980s when its language was adopted and transformed by big business. While post-modernism was not certainly unique in being sucked into a late-capitalist cycle of consumption, obsolescence and disposal, those aspects of it which drew from the pop art tradition had acknowledged the inevitability of the process from the start. An internationally understood yet culturally vacuous idiom came to dominate commercial architecture, draining post-modernism of its vitality.

The large commercial practices that had made their reputations with modern office buildings, among them Gollins Melvin Ward and Seifert, were happy to adopt post-modern classicism. Large City-fringe developments such as Broadgate and the development of London's Docklands, fast-tracked through a development corporation created in 1981 and led by first American and then Canadian developers, attracted American multi-national practices in 1986–7. These included Skidmore, Owings and Merrill (SOM), Kohn Pederson Fox and Swanke Hayden Connell; their work lacked the cutting wit and irony of the early, smaller trailblazers of the style. Certain projects of Terry Farrell and James Stirling tended towards a gross classicism, while post-modernists such as Michael Graves, Robert Stern and Arata Isozaki lost credibility by designing 'entertainment architecture' for the Disney Corporation.

When new buildings again began to be commissioned in the early 1990s, many for a revived public sector, a neo-modernism assured in its sustainability and energy efficiency took the place of post-modernism. The results suggest that many of the lessons of post-modernism had been learned – this new British modernism was more inclusive and relaxed than the old, and free to partake of wilful forms, bold colour, diverse materials and, latterly, laser-cut patterns from local sources. The gestural range of post-modernism was perpetuated in 'iconic' buildings seeking to regenerate an area, such as Will Alsop's Peckham Library of 1998–9, and as a means of expressing the ventilation pipes and turrets required by ecologically minded buildings, such as those by Alan Short and Bill Dunster.

Perhaps the widest ranging legacy of post-modernism in architecture has been its questioning of how our cities are thrown together and the creation of new pedestrian routes and public spaces. The built works of British post-modernism, always in the minority, are today fast disappearing – hence this book. But the post-modern movement's guiding principles and strategies – chief among them pluralism, context, narrative and subversion – have never been more relevant to contemporary architecture.

Staff Common Room, Glasgow School of Art, by Gillespie, Kidd & Coia, project architect
Andy MacMillan, 1981 (demolished)

Houses
and Housing

Page 22: Swedish Quays, Greenland Dock, Southwark, by Price & Cullen, 1987–8

Right: Highgate New Town, phase 2B, by Camden Architect's Department (job architects Bill Forrest and Oscar Palacio), 1978–81

N owhere was modernism deemed to have to have failed so completely in Britain as in the realm of public housing. Indeed, for many people the defining image of the Modern Movement is of ominously grey tower blocks trembling in windswept solitude, as lambasted in Britain as early as November 1967 when Nicholas Taylor wrote of the '"subjective" hatred of the tenants for the rough-shuttered concrete that is thrust upon them'.[1] Taylor was as critical of modern planning as of its architecture in a paean to low-rise, high-density housing published in 1973 as *The Village in the City*.[2] His own response was to become a local councillor and to commission Walter Segal to work with the housing waiting list on self-build homes, while under the Skeffington Report of 1969 tenants began to have a greater say in their housing. Councillors at the London Borough of Camden voted in 1976 to abandon an approved scheme for Highgate New Town, and minimalist blocks clad in asbestos cement panels were redesigned with brick walls and pitched roofs, featuring deep eaves and trelliswork, by the same project architects, Bill Forrest and Oscar Palacio. This was the bottom line for housing in the 1980s: flats that looked like houses wherever possible, built of contrasting bright shades of brick and evoking, perhaps consciously, the way young children first draw their homes.

More public housing was built in the late 1970s and early 1980s than has generally been supposed, particularly in London, but government policies in the early 1980s offered council tenants huge discounts to buy their homes, causing a reduction in the stock for rent that was never replaced. Initiative turned to the housing associations, which had grown rapidly in the 1970s, building as many homes in 1979 as they had in the whole of the 1960s, thanks to support from the Housing Corporation under the Housing Act of 1974 and from local authorities such as the Greater London Council. The movement brought together innovative young professionals and traditional charities.

From 1986 the Government supported associations' borrowing from private investors and the ending of rent controls in a bid to increase its building stock, and by the 1990s they were the dominant force in building new homes for rent. This was achieved only by significant rent rises, thrusting many existing tenants into dependence on housing benefits; in the 1990s many housing association blocks became, according to the economist Will Hutton, 'even greater sinks of the marginalized groups in society than council housing'.[3]

The model for new rented housing, across London in particular, was **St Mark's Road**, Kensington, a reinterpretation of a London terrace as flats and maisonettes with steps and chunky gate piers following the street by Jeremy and Fenella Dixon, in 1977–9. Aldo van Eyck and Theo Bosch produced similar row housing at Zwolle, Netherlands, in 1977, but the genre is strongest in Britain. Westminster City Council gave a site on Lanark Road to a developer to build low-cost housing for sale, realized in 1981–3 by the Dixons as flats resembling a line of paired early Victorian villas, the principal windows paired and set in stuccoed surrounds. Colquhoun & Miller's small infill schemes at Gaisford Street and Caversham Road, amid Victorian housing, were contextual in scale and Italianate in their details, but bright brick and Mondrian-like square details informed their housing in Milton Keynes, and an infill scheme for LB Hackney in Shrubland Road and Albion Drive, of 1984, adopted Lanark Road's idiom of a gabled semi-detached house (or 'semi'), featuring a stuccoed centrepiece set behind a single column. The influence of St Mark's Road is still more apparent in LB Islington's **Highcroft Estate**, completed in 1986 with more steps, brick gate piers and pointy blue details, while in the hands of Pollard, Thomas & Edwards stripes of brickwork on bulky, irregularly shaped blocks became the new London vernacular. Such interpretations of a London terrace look nothing like the real thing, yet are a thoroughly English and successful piece of post-modern architecture and planning in their own right.

The real boom in the 1980s was in the building of private houses and especially flats for sale, particularly to support the growing demand from London office workers. After the deregulation of the banking sector in 1986, the mortgage market became massively competitive in its methods of funding the demand for home ownership. House prices initially surged but then collapsed when interest rates rose sharply at the end of the decade, leaving many people in negative equity. Meanwhile, the British obsession with homeownership brought a new mix of modern and traditional housing to the capital.

In London, the race was on in the 1980s to find new locations convenient for the City. Nowhere was more available than Docklands, leading to schemes ranging from luxurious riverside lofts to flats for first-time buyers at Beckton, East Ham. Striped brickwork can be found all along the remains of the Western Dock, Wapping, where a narrow canal is lined with terraces by Form Design Group, Ronald Toomey & Partners, Pinchin & Kellow and Boyer Design, all from the mid- to late 1980s. Richard Reid repeated the form of the paired, linked semi at Finland Quay West on Greenland Dock in 1987–9, while nearby at The Lakes, Shepheard Epstein Hunter floated villa-like blocks (1988–90) in the remains of Norway Dock, an unusual demonstration of picturesque informality.

Behind the waterfronts more terraces recreated traditional London squares, some gated, a phenomenon previously reserved for the most exclusive parts of the West End. At Compass Point, by Jeremy Dixon/BDP for Costain Homes, of 1985–8, lines of linked villas terminate in a crescent. Coutts Crescent in Kentish Town, built by Chassay Architects in 1988, similarly has taller pavilions at either end, but here the elevations are striped and the fenestration treated as a giant order between piers. At Sutton Square, CZWG combined a small landscaped area with car parking, in one of the first schemes for a new square (1983–5) that combined terraced houses and flats set behind screen walls concealing small private gardens. The crescent even gave an unseemly grandeur to the Surrey Docks, with CZWG's Wolfe Crescent, also from 1989. A more traditional enclosed square is Ambassador Gardens, Beckton, by Form Design from 1987, where terraces ending in large, hipped-roof pavilions surround a square with benches and an obelisk.

More distinctive were individual blocks for young, small-scale developers, among them several architects. Roger Zogolovitch of CZWG set up Charterhouse Estates whose first project was Royalty Studios, 16 artists' studios and workshops in a retro factory style, completed in 1986, while Michael Baumgarten followed Horselydown Square with mixed-use developments at Bermondsey Square and Gainsborough Studios. As the supply of old warehouses for conversion into executive flats and live/work units ran out, so new ones had to be created, post-modernism assuming characteristics from homespun London architecture and its dominant lifestyles. Whereas post-war planning deliberately sought to separate housing from industrial uses, post-modernism thrust them back together, as exemplified by Jestico and Whiles's Bruges Place on the Regent's Canal, a striped smorgasbord of flats layered over light industrial units built for a local developer, Mark Fitzpatrick Estates, in 1985–6.

Outside London, the redevelopment of waterside and other derelict lands came later. The exception was Bristol, where only two industrial sites on the Floating Harbour remained in operation by 1980. Already the docks were beginning to be redeveloped for museum and leisure uses, led by one of Britain's first design-and-build companies, the enterprising JT Group. The Bristol Byzantine style of 19th century warehousing saw a natural progeny in

Finland Quay West (now 1–67 Acland Court), Greenland Dock, Southwark, by Richard Reid, 1987–9

polychrome housing and offices of varying scale, notably with the early and extensive housing at Merchants Landing, Bathurst Basin, of 1980–4, by the Ronald Toone Partnership, followed in 1986 by nearby Baltic Wharf.

James Gowan was one of the few architects to build public housing outside London in the late 1970s, with a small estate for Chelmsford Borough Council at East Hanningfield. The result was oddly formal for the genre, with an alternating rhythm of mono-pitch tiled roofs and round windows, manufactured by a firm of marine engineers. The influences were Dutch, but tuned up by classical proportions and a nod to Palladio's Villa Valmarana, where round windows serve as capitals in the implied order of the simple façade. Purer still was his single **Greenbank House** at Chester for Chaim Schreiber, completed in 1982 and a contrast to the heavyweight concrete and brick of his London town house for the same client.

Nowhere is the opportunity for individual architectural expression as great as in the private house, and no other decade is as diverse in its examples. Compared with the open planning of previous decades, houses of the 1980s are more cellular, with dedicated spaces for fine dining, office work and perhaps even a special games or television room. Amid a growing market for pure neoclassical houses, Arthur Quarmby introduced classical columns into his earth-sheltering houses, for example at Mole Manor,

Gloucestershire (1985), while Martin Johnson extended Barley Splatt, Cornwall, in a neo-Gothic style that evolved over the decade 1974–85 with the artist owners, Graham and Annie Ovenden. The owners played a larger role in the look of post-modern houses than those in other styles, most notably Charles Jencks and Maggie Keswick, who with Terry Farrell reinvented their home, Thematic House, in a true collaboration.

Many young clients preferred converting an old house to building a new one, apart from in London, where gap sites and backland plots encouraged the revival of inner-city living, as with the warehouse blocks. To build in central London, as did Janet Street-Porter in 1988, was a radical move, with the architecture again being a marriage of the local environs with distant sources, old and new. Then the race was on to find gaps, however small, in which to squeeze a house.

Modernism's problem was that individual buildings were generally more successful than large-scale planning schemes. By contrast, post-modernism was clever in tying in new development to the existing grain, accepting mixed use and the motor car in a return to more traditional streets and squares. Nowhere is this seen better than in housing, and especially in the medium-rise, high-density developments of inner London.

St Mark's Road Housing

North Kensington, London
1977–9, Jeremy and Fenella Dixon

St Mark's Road emerged out of a moment of crisis. Having spectacularly won the 1973 competition for Northamptonshire's County Hall with a design for a giant glittering pyramid, the project stalled, leaving Jeremy and Fenella Dixon in limbo. Their wider crisis was one of faith in modernism.

Kensington Housing Trust's commission of 24 houses and 20 flats prompted the Dixons' about-turn from modernist abstraction to the reinterpretation of London's street patterns and housing. Here, narrow frontage flats are paired to create broad gables, while the steps up to family dwellings and down to basement flats echo the scale and rhythm of their Edwardian neighbours. Typical of London street architecture is the gradation of privacy and possession from pavement to front door (via steps and porches) and the distinction between demonstrative front gardens and messy, individualistic backs. Behind the frontages, the plots are cranked to fit the corner site and contrive longer gardens.

The design marks a return to decoration and allusion: a collage of Victorian eclecticism, Mondrian coloured grids and Dutch crow-step gables present a cheery face to the street, while the pyramidal caps to the gate piers allude to the Northamptonshire project. St Mark's Road was exhibited at the 1980 Venice Biennale and enjoyed much subsequent influence, not least on the Dixons' subsequent Lanark Road (1981–3) and Ashmill Street (1983–5) in Maida Vale and at Compass Point on the Isle of Dogs (1984–7).

Thematic House

19 Lansdowne Walk, Holland Park, London
1979–85, Charles Jencks with Terry Farrell Partnership

Charles Jencks and his wife Maggie Keswick started in 1978 with a
half-stuccoed, mid-19th century villa. Over the course of six years, in
collaboration with Terry Farrell, they realized a built polemic on symbolic
architecture.

As is traditional, the exteriors become increasingly informal and
convivial as one moves from front to back. Yet anthropomorphic themes are
introduced in the street: the double doorknobs reflect the symmetry of the
human body, while dormers feature face motifs modestly dubbed 'Jencksiana'
(both originated in an earlier design for Keswick's apartment at Park Walk,
Chelsea). The side addition references the rusticated stucco and decorative
motifs of the adjoining houses, while the gable-end chimney stacks bear
sunburst capitals and a staggered base. Greatest licence is found in the garden
elevation, a stylized portrait of family members.

The interior is a rich amalgam of iconographic programme, decorative
scheme, artwork and bespoke furniture. The thematic layers – 'solar house'
(in which Farrell's passive solar strategy was reflected by sun motifs); 'terrace
house' (interconnected garden terraces) and 'time house' (marked by
celestial bodies) – show Jencks grappling with the challenge of how to create
a resonant symbolism in an agnostic, multicultural age. A seasonal scheme
('spring', 'summer', 'autumn' and 'winter') for the principal ground-floor
rooms was prompted by an 18th-century design by J-F Neufforge and the
couple's seasonal rhythms (they were then wintering in Los Angeles and
passing summers in London).

Architect friends were assigned rooms to design, in an architectural
equivalent of the 'exquisite corpse', a surrealist parlour game in which each
player adds to a collaborative drawing without knowing the contributions of
the others. While Jeremy Dixon and Rem Koolhaas's contributions did not
materialize, Michael Graves designed the winter and spring fireplaces and

Piers Gough created a *trompe l'oeil* Jacuzzi by inverting a Borromini dome. David Quigley, Simon Sturgis and other members of Farrell's team devised many details.

The interior was reordered using a hybrid vocabulary of shifted axes, diagonal vistas and layering. Framed views were created by opening up the house, while beams and scalloped 'London columns' maintain the identity of each room within the semi-open layout. Planning constraints prompted the spatial compression of the architectural library, with its tent-like roof and stepped floor, giving glimpses to the room below.

The seasonal rooms rotate around a spiral 'solar' staircase, whose geometry radiates into adjacent spaces. Its 52 pre-cast concrete treads are each subdivided into seven sections, marking the weeks and days, while moulded soffits are inspired by Inigo Jones's Queen's House at Greenwich. Orbs on the three aluminium rails represent the paths of the sun, earth and moon, travelling towards a mosaic representing a black hole, by Eduardo Paolozzi. On axis is the 'moonwell', a mirror-backed, semi-circular light shaft in the manner of Charles Moore's New Haven house (1966–7). Like John Soane's house or Thomas Tresham's triangular lodge, the Thematic House is an inimitable mixture of the didactic and recondite, suspended between private fantasy and public polemic.

Greenbank House

Greenbank, Eaton Road, Chester
1980–2, James Gowan with Antony MacIntyre

Gowan built a house for Chaim and Sara Schreiber in London in 1963–5, a project that precipitated his split with James Stirling. Schreiber had business interests in the north of England and, wanting a pied-à-terre suitable for meetings, had secured two plots overlooking the River Dee. Growing infirmity led him to demand a bungalow and Gowan's solution – with the living accommodation, the main bedroom and a maid's room on the ground floor, and a guest room in the roof – is a traditional suburban chalet. Gowan described the L-shaped house, which turns its back on the town, as a roof set on pilotis, made possible by a steel frame. Yet the oculus in the gable is so large and bold, and the overhang so dramatic, that the effect is of a Palladian country house in miniature. Gowan's simplest building, exploring the most basic geometries, is also a mannerist one, inspired by Rudolf Wittkower's *Architectural Principles in the Age of Humanism*, Colin Rowe's essay 'The Mathematics of the Ideal Villa' and Matila Ghyka's study of the Golden Section in her *A Practical Handbook of Geometrical Composition and Design*.

Gowan produced a second design for Chester, for accommodating visiting family members, in which round windows are accompanied by a large dining bay and a round projection for the staircase. He also produced a design for a London home planned for Schreiber's retirement, inspired by Charles Rennie Mackintosh's house at Kilmacolm, and again with an L-shaped plan. But Schreiber was taken seriously ill and neither of these designs were built; nor did he ever live at Greenbank.

16–20 Church Crescent

Hackney, London
1981–4, Colquhoun & Miller

These taut, white boxes are rich in historical allusions, articulating
Colquhoun & Miller's wide-ranging cultural interests. Commissioned by
the London Borough of Hackney, the pair of three-storey semi-detached
houses occupies a fan-shaped site adjacent to St John of Jerusalem Church.
Descendants of the architects' Two Mile Ash (1973–84) and Oldbrook 2
(1976–82) estates at Milton Keynes, their form of rendered cubes with
shallow-pitched, hipped roofs adopts that of the early 19th-century English
villa. Like stuccoed Regency houses, the render is scored with lines in
imitation of ashlar masonry construction.

Like the architects' earlier housing at Caversham Road and Gaisford
Street in Kentish Town, (1975–9), the scheme relates to the revival of stuccoed
pre-war modernism while the gridded side windows and monochrome
palette suggests C R Mackintosh and Josef Hoffman. The blind central
portion of the front elevation was prompted by Palladio's Casa Cogollo in
Vicenza. Rigorously planned yet formalist, the design mediates between
rationalist abstraction and what Colquhoun, alluding to the philosophy
of Wittgenstein, described as 'language games'. He would not have located
Church Crescent within the post-modernist canon; notwithstanding,
it illustrates the extent to which memory and self-reference permeate
Colquhoun & Miller's work.

Hillrise Road housing

Islington, London
1983–6, Islington Architect's Department under Christopher Purslow

London housing was delegated to the boroughs on local government
reorganization in 1965. Alf Head, the incoming chief architect, steered
Islington from comprehensive redevelopment to intricate, low-rise high-
density infill commissioned from the likes of Darbourne & Darke, Andrews,
Sherlock & Partners, and John Melvin. The work of Islington's in-house
designers tended towards a picturesque townscape approach of arched
windows and mews, although humour and irony sometimes broke in: the
crow-step gables of Catherine Griffiths Court (1987–8) borrow the square
tiles of Lubetkin's Finsbury Health Centre opposite.

Highcroft Estate and Belvoir Estate, twin estates to the north of the
borough, were amongst Islington's last new-build housing schemes. They
closed almost a century of London municipal housing that had started
with the Housing of the Working Classes Branch of the London County
Council. At the larger Highcroft, clumps of low dwellings were distributed
along the retained street frontages, divided by pedestrian ways and 'mixer
courts'. A range of housing types was provided but, while plans and servicing
arrangements were rationalized, a proliferation of shapes, materials and
colours sometimes obscures the divisions between dwellings. The 'Y tracery'
glazing nods towards St Mary's Church to the south.

Belvoir is a tighter, more assertive group of sheltered housing on an
awkward wedge of land to the west. The turning circles of the residents'
wheelchairs and mobility scooters cued the bold curves of the terraces and
stairs, with brickwork neatly executed in stretcher bond. James Stirling's
influence is detectable in the detailing of Mackintosh-like gridded windows,
striped stair turrets, swooping parapets, triangular-headed lintels and yellow
metal conservatories.

Architect's own house

Lisbellaw, near Enniskillen, County Fermanagh
1984, Richard Pierce

Richard Pierce is descended through seven generations of country builders, but studied architecture rather than painting only because his parents considered it a more secure career. He trained at Edinburgh College of Art and in the summer of 1964 worked in the United States, in Pennsylvania, where a fellow student introduced him to the work of Robert Venturi. Venturi's mother, Vanna, gave Pierce a VIP tour of the house newly completed for her by her son after hearing Pierce's Irish accent through the door.

This little house by Pierce is essentially one double-height space, with bedrooms packed at one end and a kitchen and storage at the other – a variant on the typical medieval plan. The plan is not evident externally, where the elevations are conventional save for window surrounds of Venetian red. Internally, the sloping roof ensures this is no modernist space but what Pierce calls 'vernacular with a twist'. There is a nod to Robert Venturi in the large segmental arch framing the big bay window, a smaller one over the fireplace to one side, and a red steel beam. Pierce also admired the way Romaldo Giurgola refined the ideas of Louis Kahn. Most striking is a semi-circular ring wall, realized in blockwork but reminiscent of an ancient Irish fort, sheltering the front of the house. The house survives little altered save that a new kitchen has been added behind the bedrooms and stair.

When Pierce built himself a larger house, at nearby Derrygonnelly in 1995, it took the form of a ruined circular fort, or cashel, in Donegal sandstone. Into this he inserted a timber structure to permit a glass wall that gives panoramic views over Lough Carrick.

Shadwell Basin housing

Maynards Quay, Wapping, London
1986–8, MacCormac Jamieson Prichard & Wright

This group of flats and houses reinforces the edge of New Shadwell Basin, built in 1854–8, pausing to acknowledge the Regency St Paul's Church. As at Compass Point (Jeremy Dixon, 1984–7) and Finland Quay West (Richard Reid, 1987–9), a continuous terrace is articulated into gabled groups. Here, however, the composition is freer with an anthropomorphic configuration of porthole windows and balconies emerging from a split gable. Study of Venetian palazzos and Telford & Hardwick's St Katharine's Dock prompted a rhythm of solid masonry relieved by glass and steel linking sections. Higher densities were obtained by adopting warehouse-style deep plans, with central kitchens and bathrooms and living rooms and bedrooms front and back. The A-B-A rhythm of the colonnade references Palladio's basilica at Vicenza and the Albert Dock in Liverpool (where James Stirling was then working on Tate Liverpool) while the metalwork details derive from the industrial vernacular of loading bays, crane cabins and gantries.

The London Docklands Development Corporation commissioned the outline design, assuming the role of client to speed up the pace of development. Minor departures from the initial 1984 scheme attest to a bumpy planning process. After local sailing groups protested about impacts on wind speeds, the Corporation insisted on two- to three-storey houses in the north-east corner and the omission of a lockside terrace to the south west. Their client then switched to another firm to prepare working drawings. Despite a slight coarsening in the execution, the design is sufficiently robust to prevail.

Mercers' House

384–400 Essex Road and 2 Mitchinson Road,
Islington, London
1991–2, John Melvin & Partners

This sheltered housing for the Mercers' Company, the oldest of the City of London's livery companies, advances a post-modernism with strong roots in English architectural history. There is a baroque sensibility to the strong perpendicular emphasis, undulating cornice and lively roofline, and affinities with Edwardian mansion blocks. Dual aspect flats are paired around three groups of staircases and lifts, step-free access being required throughout. By thrusting out the stair towers, Melvin obtains a strong vertical emphasis inspired by Louis Kahn and the earliest works of Charles Holden. Giant lunettes peep out above, more redolent of Lutyens's mannerist games than the post-modernist prototype at Venturi & Rauch's Guild House in Philadelphia.

A reinforced concrete frame, used for speed and flexibility, is clad in impeccable russet-red brickwork with white pre-cast dressings. Snapped headers simulate Flemish bond, while the two-inch bricks beloved of Edwardian builders augment the apparent scale. A giant order is implied by the chequerboard pilasters, which are carried over the cornice to form chimney-like vents. The source is Lutyens's Marsh Court, where the chequered stonework is studiedly irregular, and his Page Street flats, where the patternmaking assumes an almost Op Art scale.

Melvin lived locally and strove to recreate the ornate doorcases, handrails and fanlights he admired in the Islington buildings he witnessed being pulled down, and which rarely appeared in their replacements. Lacking stair towers, the garden elevations are closer to his earlier housing for Islington Council. The adjacent group practice surgery announces itself as an institutional building while still relating to the main block.

Landscapes

British garden design is a landscape of contradiction and complexity: the artifice of a 'naturalistic' style, the faux history of classical temples and Gothic ruins and an early interest in oriental gardens. Its inherent potential for outlandishness was recognized by Edward James (1907–84), the poet and supporter of the Surrealist movement. On inheriting West Dean House in Sussex, James engaged Christopher ('Kit') Nicholson and Hugh Casson to transform the estate's shooting lodge, Monkton House by Edwin Lutyens, into a remarkable surrealist folly. While James also added to the West Dean garden, his surreal masterwork is Las Pozas, an assemblage of huge concrete follies in a sub-tropical rainforest, located in the Sierra Madre mountains of Mexico.

The gardens of Sir Geoffrey Jellicoe (1900–96) offer a long journey into post-modernism, stimulated by Carl Jung's theories of the subconscious. At Shute House, Donhead St Mary, Wiltshire (1969–75), water from the River Nadder is channelled over a narrow rill to create a musical cascade, while Kashmiri gardens inspired a gravity-fed bubble fountain. His landscaping of the grounds of Sutton Place (1980–4), Guildford, for the American art collector Stanley Seeger was conceived as an allegory of human evolution and creation – a sequence of walled gardens culminates in a giant relief by Jellicoe's friend, Ben Nicholson, in white Carrara marble.

Little Sparta, the garden cultivated by the concrete poet Ian Hamilton Finlay (1925–2006), at Dunsyre in Scotland, evolved over decades to cover the iconography of war, the French Revolution and the classical inheritance. While Finlay rarely left his arcadia, he collaborated with many artists and installed an 'Improvement Garden' at the Stockwood Craft Museum in Luton. **The Garden of Cosmic Speculation** by Finlay's friend Charles Jencks (1939–) has functioned as a test bed for subsequent commissions at the Scottish Gallery of Modern Art, Edinburgh (1999–2002); Jupiter Artland at

Kirknewton (2003–10) and the Crawick Multiverse near Sanquhar (opened in 2015). Jencks has also designed several gardens for the Maggie's Centres founded by his late wife, Maggie Keswick, herself an authority on Chinese gardens. At Prospect Cottage, the artist and filmmaker Derek Jarman (1942–94) built up a garden of flint circles, flotsam and wild coastal plants at the shingle shore of Dungeness in Kent. The cottage itself, black tar-boarded with bright yellow sashes, adds to the scenic enigma of the place.

Roof gardens, too, lend themselves to surreal encounters and architectural fantasies – from the baroque fireplace and grass carpet of Le Corbusier's Charles de Beistegui Apartment (1929–31) to Martha Schwartz's Splice Garden (1986), an artificial hybrid of a Japanese Zen garden and a French Renaissance parterre for the microbiologists of the Whitehead Institute at Cambridge, Massachusetts. At RMC House, Surrey (1988–9), Edward Cullinan Architects with Derek Lovejoy Partnership designed an allusive roof garden atop a concrete and glass office building. Giant red and white chess pieces (a reference to Lewis Carroll's *Through the Looking-Glass*) and a gabled gazebo in homage to Philip Webb provide sources of distraction from the workplace.

Arabella Lennox-Boyd's roof garden for Stirling Wilford's **1 Poultry** combines a formal design of box ribbons, gravel and stone spheres at the building's 'prow' with a circular pergola around the central drum. A similar combination of open-air rotunda and trailing plants is evident at the Broadgate Arena (1985–7, Peter Foggo of Arup Associates), devised to serve as an open-air theatre in summer and an ice-skating rink in winter. Its travertine facing, 'ruined' southeastern quadrant and upper trellis suggest an overgrown, ruined amphitheatre. The classical formality of the landscaping at Canary Wharf, by Laurie Olin of Hanna Olin with Sir Roy Strong, reflects the transatlantic Beaux Arts approach of Skidmore, Owings & Merrill's master plan. Cabot Square and Westferry Circus (1987–91) are islanded gardens in the tradition of the London square, enlivened by public art, water features and bespoke street furniture and railings.

As well as offering amenity, parks can symbolize urban renewal. An ambitious government-funded regeneration programme was the reclamation of derelict sites for a programme of biennial garden festivals, beginning in Liverpool in 1984 and followed by Stoke-on-Trent, Glasgow, Gateshead and Ebbw Vale. But the project's gardens and sculptures proved ephemeral and only fragments survive, including a stone circle at Stoke-on-Trent and a clock, *In the Nick of Time*, for Ebbw Vale but now relocated to Newport. A 1995 design competition held by the London Docklands Development Corporation resulted in the Thames Barrier Park, completed in 2000 and featuring a skewed parterre and a huge sunken garden resembling

Saint Mary's Churchyard Park, Elephant and Castle, London, by Martha Schwartz Partners, 2007–8

a horticultural dry dock. Its designer, Alain Provost of Group Signes, was consultant to the 1992 Parc André Citroën in Paris, a Mitterrand-era *grand projet* laid out on a similarly post-industrial riverside site. More playful is Martha Schwartz's 2007–8 landscaping of St Mary's Churchyard at London's Elephant and Castle, including Belisha beacon lighting, colourful play areas and big concrete spheres embedded in grass mounds.

Little Sparta

Dunsyre, Lanarkshire, Scotland
1967–2006, Ian Hamilton Finlay

In the winter of 1966, the poet Ian Hamilton Finlay and his wife Sue arrived at Stonypath, an abandoned six-acre croft in the Pentland foothills with sheep bleating at the door. During the early 1960s he had created his first inscriptions in concrete for the garden of the couple's first house at Ardgay, Easter Ross. Seeing the possibility of creating a garden at Stonypath, Finlay diverted a small burn to create a series of ponds, naming the largest, Lochan Eck, after his son (Eck being the Scots diminutive of Alexander). In summer 1967, stone inscriptions carved by Maxwell Allan were embedded in a sunken garden, soon to be joined by a sundial, *Four Seasons in Sail*. Finlay's collaborations with letter-cutters, stonemasons and other skilled craftspeople reflected a determination to realize his work to the highest standards.

Over the next half century Finlay created more than 275 works that included inscriptions, sculpture, garden features and architectural elements; all intertwined with their landscape setting. With *Nuclear Sail* (1973), beside Lochan Eck, and the aircraft carriers of *Homage to the Villa d'Este*, warship imagery began to subsume the fishing boats of his early poetry. The re-naming of the garden as 'Little Sparta' in 1979 (alluding to Edinburgh's epithet, the Athens of the North) and of the garden temple to 'Apollo' (c.1982) chimed with the post-modern reclamation of the classical style. A 20th-century *ferme ornée*, the garden was for Finlay a place both of self-elected exile and cultural resistance – he wrote, 'Certain gardens are described as retreats when they are really attacks'.[1]

Garden of Cosmic Speculation

Portrack, Dumfries
1988–, Charles Jencks and Maggie Keswick

Maggie Keswick's childhood was spent between the Far East, where her father Sir John traded, and Portrack House, their home on the Scottish borders. After completing the garden of the **Thematic House**, her home with Charles Jencks in London, her thoughts turned to the grounds at Portrack. From the 1986 'Foster, Rogers, Stirling' exhibition at the Royal Academy of Arts, the couple acquired Stirling's full-scale mock-up of elements from the **Neue Staatsgalerie** in Stuttgart. Re-erected in Portrack's Crow Wood, and with Jencks's addition of a screen-cum-stair, it was christened The Nonsense. Dredging a mosquito-infested lake, they had the idea of using the excavated soil to form a serpentine landform, in counterpoint to the new waterway, as if water and land dragons were embracing. The first of several sinuous earth mounds, it echoed the rolling hills around Portrack and also Maggie's interest in Chinese gardens. After her death in 1995 the garden continued to grow as Jencks used nature and the senses to explore a growing interest in cosmology through collaborations with craftspeople, artists and scientists, and with head gardener, Alistair Clarke. A cascade of steps and water tells the story of the universe while sculptures inspired by the DNA helix are discovered inside a walled kitchen garden, and the Black Hole Terrace and Quark Walk celebrate complexity science. A sense of human achievement is contributed by the railway garden that commemorates worthies of the Scottish Enlightenment.

Civic
Buildings

here is far more civic architecture from the late 20th century than might initially be supposed. It is also very diverse, since numerous sources of funding were explored in place of the government subsidies that had supported building works since World War II. The Labour Government introduced cash limits on local government expenditure in 1976, which were tightened by the Conservatives after they won the 1979 election. Private investors and large companies sponsored not only art exhibitions but also buildings, while universities explored more vigorously the North American practice of seeking endowments from their alumni. The results were eclectic.

The reorganization of local government into larger units, in London in 1965 and elsewhere in 1974, required many authorities to assimilate scattered offices into one efficient organization. In Hillingdon, local councillors rejected a modernist design as early as 1971, and Andrew Derbyshire of Robert Matthew, Johnson-Marshall & Partners turned to the Arts and Crafts traditions of his native Hertfordshire in producing complex brick elevations and pitched roofs. Largely built in 1973–7, the building marked the first major reaction in Britain by a modernist architect in favour of overtly historicist elevations. It caught the mood of the times, and critics responded excitedly.

More neo-vernacular brick designs with big roofs followed, as at Hadleigh, Suffolk, where Arup Associates built offices for Babergh District Council in 1977–82. Michael Innes of Lambert Scott & Innes adopted a similar idiom with a plan of irregular hexagons at South Norfolk House, Long Stratton, in 1978–9. At the more formal Pippbrook, council offices for Mole Valley, Dorking, built in 1981–4, the combination of octagons with bell-cast-like roofs and bold geometric shapes is more identifiably post-modern. Faulkner-Brown Hendy Watkinson Stonor's civic centre at Chester-le-Street (1981–2, demolished in 2014) was a clean-cut high-tech building of mirror

Hillingdon Civic Centre, designed in 1971 by Andrew Derbyshire of Robert Matthew, Johnson-Marshall & Partners, built 1973–7

glass, but its central arched arcade made reference to the Crystal Palace, appropriate since this was a public mall. The most strikingly post-modern civic centre by British architects was built at Mississauga, Canada, in 1982–6 by Edward Jones and Michael Kirkland, following a competition where James Stirling was among the assessors. The influence of Léon Krier and Aldo Rossi in the massive pedimented block, drum and tower was more palpable than in anything realized in Britain, while a pyramid roof to the central hall recalled Dixon and Jones's unrealized scheme for Northamptonshire County Hall of 1973.

More earnestly British is Northampton Guildhall, where there is a telling contrast between a comprehensive yet deferential restoration by Roderick Gradidge of E W Godwin's great hall and council chamber of 1861–4, and an extension of 1989–91 by local architects Stimpson Watson Bond, which picks up the proportions, rhythm and stone cladding of the original façade in a simplified design on a steel frame. A complex marriage of old and new was accomplished at the City of London Guildhall, where the bombed-out 15th-century hall was restored and extended by Sir Giles Gilbert Scott and his son Richard; the latter adding, in 1994–9, the Guildhall Art Gallery, with canted arches and blocks of geometric tracery shielding the double-height windows.

The rationalization of the public estate also led to new police and fire stations, of which the most eclectic was the fire station in Upper Street, Islington, designed by Peter J Smith in 1992 with rusticated columns and blue triangular oriels, almost a London vernacular by that date. More dramatic was the Government's programme of new court buildings, begun in the 1970s. The apogee was Truro's Courts of Justice, built in 1986–8 by Evans and Shalev, where over-scaled classical details are combined with glass bricks to give a quiet dignity to the three courts, a generous central space and outdoor areas. The law courts at Newcastle upon Tyne, by the Napper Collerton Partnership from 1984–90, gain dignity from a giant order and sandstone cladding, with details from nearby public buildings, yet a central glazed lift tower makes the steel frame clearly apparent beneath the overlying references. Visually uneasy but clearheaded in its planning, it led to further commissions for courts at Sheffield and Bradford.

Smaller in scale but equally assertive is an extension to Finsbury Barracks, City Road, Islington, by Arnold & Boston from 1993–4 and linking it to the older Armoury House. While the extension is far simpler and more geometric than William Whitfield's **Richmond House**, it offers a similar solution to the question of context through the use of contrasts of shapes and materials. A spectacularly formal government building is Quarry House, Leeds, designed by BDP in association with Norwest Holst construction as part of an unrealized master plan by Terry Farrell, with its grand curved stone centrepiece, and a scale and symmetry that beg comparison with Farrell's **SIS Building** in London.

The only universities with extensive building programmes in the 1980s were Oxford and, to a lesser extent, Cambridge. Here a pragmatic balance was found between modernism and romanticism. Oxford was dominated by the work of MacCormac, Jamieson and Pritchard, beginning with a scheme at Worcester College sponsored by the Sainsbury family, where a plan and overall treatment inspired by Louis Kahn was realized in 1980–2, with details indebted to the Cotswolds Arts and Crafts movement. More eclectic works followed with the Bowra Building at Wadham College (1992) and especially the Garden Quad at St John's College (1992–4), replete with an underbelly of semi-basement shared spaces reminiscent of Soane. Demetri Porphyrios won a competition in 1991 for Magdalen College that combined Gothic vernacular study bedrooms and crenelated towers with a lean, classical basilica for the Grove Auditorium built in 1997–9. At Cambridge, Porphyrios paid homage to Tudor Renaissance classicism with Ann's Court, Selwyn College, won in competition in 1996 and partly realized in 2003–9. Outside Oxbridge, Alan Short followed his engineering building at **Leicester De Montfort University** with adaptations of two theatres, in 1999 for Manchester University and in 2002–3 the Lichfield Garrick, where the thick brick insulating walls and exhaust stacks are again boldly articulated.

The first competition for extending the **National Gallery** on the Hampton site, in 1982, included an enabling development of offices. Already the rebuilding of the Mermaid Theatre by Richard Seifert and Partners, which made reference to the warehouse previously on the site behind a classical frontage, had shown in 1981 how difficult it was to combine two elements. Offices were also originally intended to fund the remodelling and extension of the Royal Opera House by Jeremy Dixon and Edward Jones, until the National Lottery, introduced in 1994, instead provided financial support. The scheme encapsulates the whole post-modernist movement, both in its 16-year gestation from 1984 onwards and in its mix of old and new: two listed buildings were remodelled and the surrounding city block rebuilt, with a new arcade in the tradition of Inigo Jones's original scheme for Covent Garden that combines ground-floor shops with facilities for the opera and ballet companies, and the audience, above. The arcade was realized in the final scheme but more post-modernist elements including a rooftop pyramid and corner drum were superseded.

Robert Venturi in 1987 celebrated 'the Art Museum as the archetypal building type of our time … the cathedral of today'.[1] In the 1970s the conversion of a warehouse to a gallery or theatre had been a means of enticing people into a derelict industrial area and stimulating new uses for the adjoining buildings. But by the 1980s new buildings for the arts were used to revitalize whole town centres, as when Venturi, Scott Brown & Associates built the new Seattle Art Museum in the heart of downtown, to reconnect art with day-to-day life and attract more visitors. During this period the art museum became a destination in its own right, fulfilling functions once led by the town hall and assembly room. The ratio of gallery to other uses in 19th-century museums was 9:1; in the 1980s it was 1:2, as space was sought for educational activities, a shop and restaurant. Within the galleries, the hessian-backed displays intended to focus attention on the art now gave way to a historically informed approach that preferred rich, red walls – approaches led by Michael Jaffé at the Fitzwilliam Museum in Cambridge and Timothy Clifford at Manchester City Art Gallery and stimulating a protracted debate between James Stirling and the Tate curators over the decoration of the **Clore Gallery** at Tate Britain.

The first new European gallery to become a destination in its own right was Richard Rogers and Renzo Piano's Georges Pompidou Cultural Centre, opened in 1977. By contrast, German museums were at the forefront of early post-modernism, beginning with Hans Hollein's Abteiberg Museum, Mönchengladbach in 1972–82, a series of semi-submerged cubes and a large-scale precursor of Stirling's approach to his tight site at the Stuttgart **Neue Staatsgalerie**. Hollein followed with the Museum for Modern Art of 1982–91 in Frankfurt, where a clutch of museums defined the stylistic conflicts of the times. In Britain, the paramount new gallery outside London was Tate St Ives, won in competition by Evans & Shalev in 1989 and opened in 1993, designed around a giant drum that echoed the shape of the gas holder formerly on the site.

The few wholly new churches of the 1980s included St Mary Magdalen, Penwortham, Preston, built in 1987–8, and St Christopher, Blackpool, of 1989–91, both by Francis Roberts in an Arts and Crafts idiom. Other church building comprised the reconstruction of those damaged or destroyed by fire, such as St Mary's, Barnes, where Edward Cullinan felt he was reviving the tradition of William Morris and Red House.[2] At the boundary of Arts and Crafts idiom and classical traditions lies William Whitfield's chapter house added to St Alban's Cathedral in 1980–2. There have been still fewer mosques of architectural interest, the exception being the Ismaili Centre, London, built in 1979–85 by Neville Conder, a modernist who here assembled a marriage of Eastern and Western motifs within an intricate granite box.

The civic buildings beg the question as to whether there is in fact a British post-modern style, when many buildings adopted the Arts and Crafts revival or the mannerisms of Charles Rennie Macintosh. Set against this gentle synthesis, the influence of Aldo Rossi, Léon Krier and Mario Botta is striking in such one-off projects as **Church of St Paul, Haringey, Newnham College**'s Rare Books Library and **Epping Forest Civic Offices**. Their abstracted European classicism is very different from the search for local references and context that is key to much British post-modernism.

Katharine Stephen Room

Rare Books Library, Newnham College, Sidgwick Avenue, Cambridge
1981–2, Joanna van Heyningen and Birkin Haward

In her first important commission, Joanna van Heyningen created a tiny jewel box, a Renaissance wayside *tempietto*. Newnham's alumnae have a strong literary tradition, celebrated in their library's collection of rare books and artefacts, and the building makes a statement to the street about the College's history, in the absence of a chapel. Brick was chosen for security and fire protection as well as acknowledging the surrounding buildings, which are mostly in the Queen Anne style by Basil Champneys. The shape and narrow site is reminiscent of Santa Maria dei Miracoli in Venice, while the striped brick harks to northern Italy as referenced in buildings like Mario Botta's house at Ligornetto of 1975–6.

Inside is a single room ringed by a gallery, all in steel. The College's first library, by Champneys from 1896–8, has a barrel-vaulted roof and a gallery with a metal balustrade; van Heyningen's building repeats these forms to create a traditional vaulted library hidden within a traditional façade. Natural light is a feature, albeit strictly limited, thanks to doll's house windows at the ends and a translucent skylight.

The library was designed before van Heyningen and Haward formed a formal practice, having met and married when working for Foster Associates in 1970. James Stirling admired the building because 'it has achieved an incredible presence, which to me is the definition of monumental'.[3] The subliminal historical references place it firmly in the European post-modern canon.

Pencadlys Cyngor Gwynedd (County Hall)

Castle Street and Shirehall Street, Caernarfon
1982–6, Merfyn H Roberts and Terry Potter of the County
Architect's Department with Dewi-Prys Thomas

Dewi-Prys Thomas (1916–85) was a charismatic and inspirational teacher, a Welsh nationalist, pacifist and sometime actor. As head of the School of Architecture in Cardiff, he argued for a Welsh tradition in design, although his own buildings (all designed before his appointment in 1960) were modern. The county hall lies deep in the walled city, hard by Caernarfon Castle, with its symbolic associations to Imperial Rome and Constantinople. For Thomas, no castle was more powerful. Despite illness and the stress of university politics, he believed it was his destiny to accept the challenge, in 1980, of producing a design for his former students.

The building's planning and massing, weaving in and out of ancient buildings, was already established, as a series of shallow floor plates between two streets with linked pedestrian and service courtyards. Yet his associates were shocked at Thomas's solution with its stepped façades, hipped roofs, arcades and random architectural incidents. However, in his early teaching days at Liverpool, sharing a flat with Colin Rowe, author of *Collage City*, he had come to recognize this changing spirit in architecture. The style befitted the town, although few origins for the various details could be sourced – Thomas had worked with Clough Williams-Ellis salvaging buildings for Portmeirion, and a balcony detail resembles one rescued from the Liverpool Sailors' Home. The heaviness of the squat columns along Shirehall Street contrasts with render elsewhere, and a mix of North German and 1950s Scandinavian pastiche is glossed with paper-thin walls and square window surrounds reminiscent of Charles Moore's Rodes House in Los Angeles (1976–9).

Richmond House

Whitehall, City of Westminster
1982–4, Whitfield Associates; listed Grade II* in 2015

Richmond House is a contextual scheme that knits together urban fabric with tact, bravery and wit. Yet like the nearby Queen Elizabeth II Conference Centre and Portcullis House, its origins lie in Sir Leslie Martin's 1965 proposal for the redevelopment of Whitehall. When government commitment to the Martin plan flagged, a programme of rebuilding and refurbishment was agreed upon. William Whitfield was appointed to overhaul the block between the Cenotaph and the Norman Shaw and Curtis Green former police buildings on Victoria Embankment. He drew upon an early fascination with castles, seeing the Shaw building as the keep and the houses along Parliament Street and Richmond Terrace as the curtain wall against which he built.

The retained structures were connected with a 'crust', in which colour, textures and forms coalesce to match their neighbours.[4] The escape stairs and service ducts were designed as towers whose 'streaky bacon' red brick and stone courses echo the Shaw building. Fine interiors reference C R Mackintosh and also Lutyens, designer of the Cenotaph. After work had started on site, Whitfield was asked to amend his design to include a Whitehall entrance. He formed a recessed entrance range, emphasizing the vertical circulation and services to create a set of strongly modelled Perpendicular towers, enhanced with rich mouldings and polychromy. He cited the lost Holbein and King Street Gates as design cues, although comparisons were inevitably drawn with the Palace of Westminster.

Epping Forest Civic Offices

High Street, Epping, Essex
1985–90, Richard Reid

Epping is on the London Underground's Central Line but nevertheless remains a market town with a real high street. Richard Reid won a competition for a civic centre for the district council, assessed by Piers Gough. He had opened a practice only in 1984, following years spent as an architectural critic and teaching at Kingston and South Bank polytechnics. The building is dominated by a toy-like red brick tower that acknowledges that of G F Bodley's church of St John the Baptist nearby. The remaining building relates to its surroundings and the scheme incorporates a 19th-century house to one side. Entrance is made either under the tower into a high, narrow atrium or via a grand ceremonial stair into the horseshoe-shaped council chamber that projects towards the street in front of it. While the effect is toy-like, it is also humane. The high, narrow atrium is of the greatest interest, where red and cream blocks are punched through with windows and openings so members of staff never feel far from the community they serve. The council chamber is traditionally formal, as is the panelled mayoral suite and members' room on the upper floor where the fenestration is boldest.

Reid gave his sources as Louis Kahn, H H Richardson and C H Townsend, with an understanding of Camillo Sitte and Gordon Cullen in the way the building brings the High Street to a close.

Bishop Wilson Memorial Library

Bishops' Primary School, Chelmsford, Essex
1985–6, Colin St John Wilson & Partners

This child-scaled library offered Sandy Wilson a diversion during the protracted design of the British Library. It bears the name of his father, Henry Wilson, Bishop of Chelmsford from 1929 to 1950 and known as 'the red bishop' for his support of the Republican cause in the Spanish Civil War. The rest of the school was designed by Thomas, Mowle & Chisnall in consultation with Wilson.

Wilson reached for a symbolic architecture in response to the library's memorializing role and suburban setting. The exterior, a drum of banded brickwork under a conical lantern, suggests two typologies: the round library (such as the Radcliffe Camera in Oxford and Sydney Smirke's British Library Reading Room) and centrally planned Roman mausolea (such as the Mausoleo di Santa Costanza in Rome).

The playful interior combines Soane-like modulated light with glossy, primary colours. Small reading groups are sheltered by an octagonal canopy projecting into the lantern. This pressed steel aedicule is painted deep blue and pierced with the 12 constellations of the zodiac, illuminated by the oculus overhead. It recalls John Summerson's essay on the aedicule: 'It is symbolism – of a fundamental kind, expressed in terms of play'.[5] For all its fun and colour, the library bespeaks its civic function and the communitarian ethics of its designer and dedicatee.

National Gallery Extension (the Sainsbury Wing)

Pall Mall East and Whitcomb Street, City of Westminster
1988–91, Venturi, Scott Brown & Associates (VSBA)

Robert Venturi and Denise Scott Brown won a competition in 1986 for an extension funded by the Sainsbury family after the Prince of Wales secured the rejection of a modernist scheme incorporating offices. The prominent site on Trafalgar Square was sensitive and modernism was out of fashion. The six competition entrants from Britain and the USA were all post-modernists.

VSBA's challenge was to design an extension that respected William Wilkins's 19th-century façade, yet was inventive. Where their new building projects forward, it repeats the old building's pilasters, but as part of a stone screen that appears wrinkled like old parchment; Venturi liked the way Wilkins's pilasters look bunched up when seen from the side. The extension unwinds down the street – openings get larger, pilasters fewer and mouldings to intervening blind windows die away. The gate piers have Art Deco capitals; the elevation up Whitcomb Street unashamedly accepts its loading bays, and the rear of the building features over-scaled stone supergraphics, which are also found inside.

The interior has the sobriety of an ancient Italian museum, dark and cavernous below galleries full of light. The link is a giant staircase that broadens as it rises, repeating that at the architects' earlier Seattle Art Museum but providing both a simple plan that can cope with huge numbers of people and a visual link with Trafalgar Square. The galleries themselves are modestly scaled to suit the delicate paintings, arranged as three enfilades set off a skewed main axis that links the extension to the main galleries, detailed in Florentine *pietra serena* sandstone.

Church of St Paul

Wightman Road, Haringey, London
1989–93, Peter Jenkins of Peter Inskip and Peter Jenkins

On Ash Wednesday 1984, Father John Seeley noticed smoke billowing out of the flèche of his Victorian church. The fire blazed overnight, leaving a gutted shell. Peter Jenkins described its replacement as 'monolithic in miniature'.[6] Taking as points of reference a 700 BC terracotta model of a shrine at the Heraion of Argos and Aldo Rossi's 1965 Monument to the Partisans at Segrate, outside Milan, St Paul's reduces the temple form to its geometric essence. Instead of a portico, the entrance is screened by two triangular towers that are like the opening to a cave. The zinc-clad triangle of the roof floats above its supports and is thrust forward, like the Tuscan pediment of Inigo Jones's St Paul's Church, Covent Garden.

The building's plan stresses the axial processional route of the High Anglican liturgy, in contrast to the centralized plan of, say, St Paul's, Bow Common. The compressed space of the narthex opens onto a tall, narrow, white-painted brick box. A sense of human scale and outward views are withheld, creating a numinous and introverted space. Light filters from the gables, augmented by tall side windows tucked behind the western towers. Square windows pierce the flank walls, just above head height and concealed from the congregation's view. Attention is instead focused on Steven Cox's free-standing altar and font of black Egyptian porphyry and travertine reredos. Small but of powerful presence, St Paul's conveys the mysteries of faith through rational means.

National Museum of Scotland

Chambers Street, Edinburgh
1996–8, Benson & Forsyth

Benson & Forsyth won an international competition for the Museum of Scotland in 1991. The museum adjoins Edinburgh's 19th-century Royal Museum and in 2008 the two collections were unified as the National Museum of Scotland. Like Enric Miralles' Scottish Parliament building, the commission was a symbol of a renewed national identity.

Benson & Forsyth started out in London at Camden Council, designing white housing estates that evoked the heroic period of modernism. At Edinburgh they endowed an abstract architectural idiom with layers of meaning. The simple, strong forms of the exterior reference Scottish castles and C R Mackintosh's Glasgow Art School: a white rendered keep rises from the confines of a curtain wall finished in orangey-pink Clashach sandstone. Entering through a free-standing drum tower, the visitor progresses into a narrow entrance hall and from there to the full-height Hawthornden Court. Display cases and narrow embrasures are built into the thick walls, bringing shafts of light into the building.

Rejecting the idea of a museum as a neutral cultural storehouse, the Museum's trustees sought a building that would animate the objects it contained. The architects used symbolism and spatial narrative to establish an architectural setting for the collections. Like the Soane Museum, it is difficult to tell where architecture ends and curatorial interpretation begins. A chronological route takes in a crypt-like basement, main galleries based on a baronial hall and an industrial machine hall. A boat-like roof terrace, based on Le Corbusier's Governor's Palace at Chandigarh, allows visitors to reconnect with Edinburgh's landscape and climate.

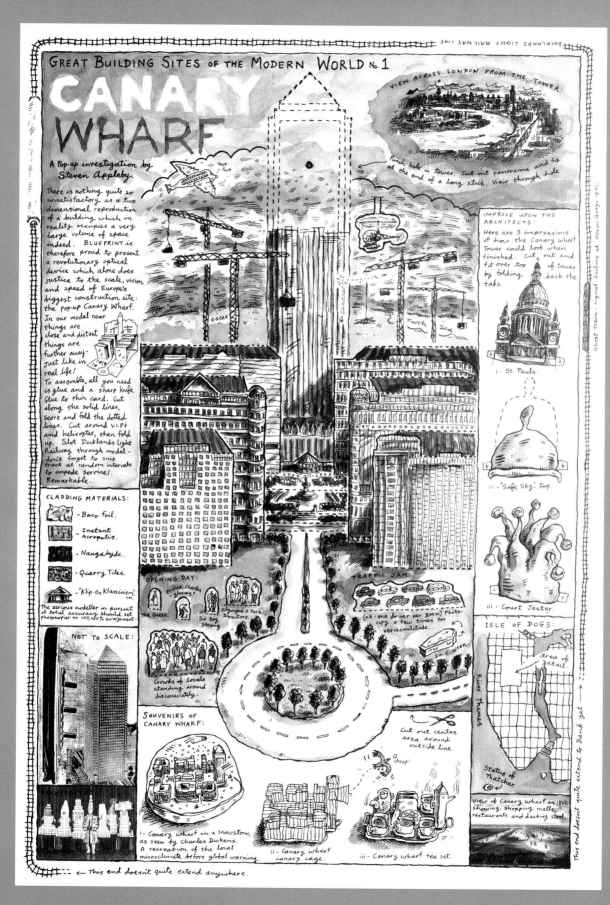

Commercial Buildings

Page 82: 'Canary Wharf' by Steven Appleby, published in *Blueprint* magazine in July 1990

Patterns of work and trade were revolutionized in the late 20th century and the commercial building played a central role both in spearheading innovation and representing an image of change. Widespread car ownership and the expansion of transport infrastructure since the 1960s had made possible new locations and building types, such as the business park, conference centre and the out-of-town shopping mall. The relocation or rebuilding of corporate headquarters at prestigious greenfield sites assumed a classicizing symmetry at the NFU **Mutual** headquarters and **Legal and General House**.

Commercial development spread beyond the traditional 'central business district' to fringe and satellite locations around transport hubs. The business park brought the prestige and amenities of the out-of-town office to a broader range of firms. Evolving from trading estates and science parks, business parks offered easy access to transport hubs and landscaped surroundings. One of the earliest examples was Aztec West, outside Bristol. CZWG's **200–260 Aztec West** and John Outram Associates' **1200 Park Avenue** presented alternatives to the predominant high-tech idiom.

The scarcity of land in central London led to the construction of US-style 'air rights' developments raised over rail tracks and termini, following the unpropitious example of Birmingham New Street station's rebuild in the 1960s. Terry Farrell's **Embankment Place** (1987–90) is the most notable example of the genre, while **Alban Gate** (1988–92) straddles a road junction. The transformation of London's Docklands, including the secondary financial district of Canary Wharf and much wharfside housing, was brought about through the London Docklands Development Corporation.

Deregulation by the Conservative government of Margaret Thatcher had major implications. Exchange controls were abolished in 1979 and the 'Big Bang' of October 1986 liberalized trading controls, permitting dealing

'Trim trail' at Aztec West business park, by Bruce Gilbreth Architects, c.1984

from screens instead of face-to-face interaction on the trading floor. The measures consolidated London's position as a global trading hub, resulting in a dramatic increase in market activity, the relocation of foreign investment banks and the growth of the financial services sector. These developments had the greatest impact on the City of London – as evidenced by its skyline – but also contributed to the growth of secondary financial centres such as Leeds, Manchester and Canary Wharf.

Market mergers gave rise to large financial services conglomerates that needed a certain type of workspace: broad, unobstructed trading floors, large floor-to-ceiling heights and abundant servicing provision. They took advantage of the 'groundscraper', a crouching form with deep and flexible interiors developed in the 1970s (an early example being Aldgate House of 1971–6 by Fitzroy Robinson & Partners). Service cores were pushed to the perimeter, freeing up space for a central atrium that was sometimes linked to an impressive entrance sequence. The Gothic **Minster Court** incorporates three dealer floors and the London Underwriting Centre (a trading hub for the insurance market) while the brassy atrium of Lansdowne House at Berkeley Square (Chapman Taylor Partners, 1985–8) pays homage to American hotel architect John Portman.

Commercial buildings are early adopters of technological innovation, from electric lifts to air-conditioning, tall buildings to ATM machines. Post-war innovations enabled prefabricated components to be assembled rapidly and safely. Lighting, heating and ventilation services along with power and communications cables were threaded through riser ducts, suspended ceilings and raised access floors. As buildings became larger and more complex, responsibility for their construction was contracted out to an army of specialists: structural, mechanical and electrical engineers; facilities managers and space planners; interior and landscape designers;

and project managers and management contractors. British developers such as Stuart Lipton and Geoffrey Wilson imported American concepts including 'shell and core' (where the developer provides a flexible framework that the tenants' contractors fit out to their client's specification) and fast-track construction (overlapping build phases that had previously been executed in sequence).

These things presented architects with both a crisis and an opportunity. As the assembly of a building became more specialized and segregated, new procurement routes forced the architectural profession to re-examine its place in the construction pecking order. Peter Foggo and Rab Bennetts of Arup Associates, embarking upon the design of Finsbury Avenue for Stuart Lipton, were warned by Kevin Roche that working for developers was like designing the wrapper on a chocolate bar. Yet entrepreneurial architects happily assembled a package for their clients, as when Terry Farrell assigned separate teams to work on the urban context, internal planning and architectural design of Embankment Place.

By the 1980s the standard template for large speculative developments was a curtain wall of stone or glass hung off a steel frame. In his proposal for Mansion House Square, a 1960s project revived in the 1980s, Mies van der Rohe used applied I-beams to signify the underlying structural order but, with equal logic, façades could allude to their non-loading bearing nature. This became increasingly the case as thinner claddings became available, including Italian stone-cutting technology that made it possible to mount thin slivers of stone onto a metal frame. At the Broadgate development, Foggo designed screens of pink granite on edge, hung in front of a glass curtain wall. The granite curtain never touches the ground, emphasizing its suspended nature. Adding post-modern irony to a similar detail, RHWL's Procession House at Ludgate Circus features clip-on rustication hung forward of an inner skin. Where the plane was simply treated as a blank canvas, the result had a graphical quality that could be seen at Ian Pollard's **Marco Polo House** and **Homebase** store; the latter even included the zigzag symbol for a break line, used by draftsmen since the 19th century.

One of the earliest signs of a backlash against the tabula rasa tendencies of modernism was the conservation movement, responding to legislation enacting the listing of buildings and the designation of conservation areas. The first conservation areas in the City of London were designated in 1971 and a resurvey in 1980–1 brought 21 new or expanded areas. A turning point was Covent Garden, where community action brought about a more sensible approach on the part of the Greater London Council and Terry Farrell's **Comyn Ching** demonstrated the possibilities of creative refurbishment. Farrell was an early advocate for what would today be termed a sustainable approach to the historic environment, rehabilitating

Tobacco Dock and devising an alternative scheme for Mansion House Square with the campaign group SAVE Britain's Heritage. At major sites, controversy reigned over the format and style of new development, as at Paternoster Square.

As a reaction to conservationism, historical pastiche often disappointed, falling between the stools of post-modern irony and the earnestness of the classical revival (although this did not stop Robert Adam trying his hand at a classical skyscraper). At worst it led to a debased version of the picturesque approach advocated by the *Architectural Review* and published by Gordon Cullen as *Townscape* in 1961. This was criticized by Jonathan Meades in 1980 as 'the new mansardism and the new orielism [...] an attempt to put [a] human face on big business'.[1] An early essay in contextual post-modernism was No. 68 Cornhill of 1981–3, where Dick Dickinson of the Rolfe Judd Group combined Vienna Secession references (the client was the Girozentrale Vienna bank) with careful attention to the string courses and cornices of its listed neighbours. The same practice's No. 62–4 Cornhill (1987–9) has a density of detail that approaches its Edwardian baroque model.

The primitive, abstract classicism that came to characterize the language of commerce in the 1980s paid scant attention to the niceties of context. Several explanations can be offered for the success of the commercial strain of post-modernism, for which Charles Jencks reserved the derogatory appellation 'PoMo'.[2] It stood for something new, a reaction to modernism appealing to popular taste, while providing a formal language easily graspable by an architect untrained in the orders and legible by clients and planning committees. Classical symmetry and a tripartite composition of base, giant order and set-back could unify the most bulky structures and relate the building to the pedestrian realm and planners' height restrictions. Its flatness, repetition and machine finishes expressed an inherited modernity in the form of fast-track programmes and prefabricated construction techniques.

From the work of Robert Venturi, Michael Graves and Charles Moore, post-modern classicism derived an elemental vocabulary of oversize motifs: voided keystones, bold Egyptianate cornices and the emergence of a shallow bow or arch from a nibbled central bay. In place of dense ornament or craft elements, visual interest was enhanced by polychromy, a suit-and-tie palette of pastel pink, grey and cornflower-blue and the texture of flamed or rusticated granite – what Stuart Lipton called 'bankers' stone'.[3] Like the revival of the North American Shingle style, the idiom was sufficiently free or impure to tolerate squat proportions and could absorb Art Deco or high-tech trimmings with ease, if not grace.

While the transatlantic derivation of commercial post-modernism chimed with the prevailing influence of North American capitalism, it did not preclude the admixture of European architectural history, whether Claude-Nicolas Ledoux, Adolf Loos or Aldo Rossi. The arrival of American commercial architects in London was marked in earnest by the 1985 Canary Wharf masterplan by Bruce Graham of the Chicago office of Skidmore, Owings & Merrill (SOM) and I M Pei (project architect Henry Cobb) for a US consortium led by G Ware Travelstead and completed by the Canadian firm Olympia & York. Graham's 25 Cabot Square in Canary Wharf (completed in 1991), along with the later phases of the Broadgate complex along Bishopsgate, revived the late 19th-century steel-framed vocabulary of Chicago architects such as Louis H Sullivan, Burnham & Root and Holabird & Roche.

In retrospect it is possible to see that the co-option of post-modern classicism by the mainstream corporate practices – SOM, Kohn Pedersen Fox, Gollins Melvin Ward, RHWL – locked it into a cycle of consumerism and over-production. It had, as Charles Jencks remarked, succumbed to its own success; post-modernism, Jencks wrote, was 'conceived as a minority approach, an oppositional movement, not a ruling style. Once it makes peace with the dominant powers, it loses direction. Thus the reflective turn within post-modernism against its own ersatz'.[4]

Little of 1980s commercial post-modernism was high art. Much could be considered the architectural equivalent of George Orwell's 'good bad book', in 1945 describing *Uncle Tom's Cabin* as 'an unintentionally ludicrous book, full of preposterous melodramatic incidents; it is also deeply moving and essentially true; it is hard to say which quality outweighs the other'.[5] Some of the most spirited examples of the idiom are not the towering monuments to mammon but the modest infill jobs run up on tight budgets or short leases: No. 8 City Road (Douglas Paskin, 1988); No. 125 Finsbury Pavement (the Halpern Partnership, c.1990) or Nos. 19–20 Noel St, Soho (Graham Moss Associates, 1987–9). See them while you can.

NFU Mutual HQ

Tiddington Road, Stratford-upon-Avon
1982–4, Robert Matthew, Johnson-Marshall & Partners
(RMJM; Alan Crawshaw, partner in charge)

Having shown they could use Arts and Crafts-style brickwork convincingly at Hillingdon Civic Centre, onetime functionalists RMJM evolved a modern classicism that personified the bespoke headquarters of the 1980s. This was a purposeful architecture, muscular and well made as befitted the merger of two companies with deep local roots seeking to express their dependability in Bath stone. It compares with Arup Associates' contemporary work in its use of geometry, but RMJM featured fat mouldings and, internally, trabeated ceilings supported on unmoulded columns, with a broad central staircase – features to give NFU Mutual a greater solidity.

The logical plan expresses the central conference room and top-floor boardroom as apses – one large and blind, one small and glazed – in the rear façade. This is long and not quite symmetrical, but its grid is so resolutely regular as to suggest the influence of Giuseppe Terragni as well as Adolf Loos. On the entrance front the top-floor drum was originally countered by a pyramidal topknot and triangular entrance canopy, the latter now removed and the original porch enclosed. To entice its staff out of town, the new building also offered generous sports facilities and a good canteen. It was furthermore one of the first large office buildings to embrace energy efficiency through heat retention and night cooling, with internal courtyards and opening windows preferred to air-conditioning. The windows were updated in 2016–17, with better insulation, cross ventilation and blinds relocated internally.

Legal and
General House

St Monica's Road, Kingswood, Banstead, Tadworth, Surrey
1986–91, Arup Associates

The Palladian high-tech of Legal and General House relates to Arup
Associates' Canons Marsh, Bristol (1989–91) and their unrealized
masterplan for Paternoster Square (1987), next to St Paul's Cathedral in the
City of London. Its setting, however, is very different: a green-belt estate on
the North Downs, hemmed in by home-counties suburbia. Avoiding the low
profile of their 1975–8 Central Electricity Generating Board headquarters,
conceived as an extension of its Bedminster Down site, the architects now
opted for a formal relationship with the rolling estate landscape, reaching for
the analogy of the classical country house.

Six office pavilions, framed by corner service towers, make a double
courtyard plan. The axial, symmetrical composition is emphasized by a
formal approach from the estate entrance to a grand central rotunda of
brick and stone. The glass envelope of the offices is sun-screened by a free-
standing colonnade linked by a continuous pergola of timber screens. A
rustic order comprises pre-cast drums supporting a notional capital of
flared timber struts and a slender cornice. That this fastidious mixture of
refined engineering and Beaux-Arts classicism followed on the heels of Arup
Associates' Broadgate phases 1–4 (1985–7) demonstrates the extent to which
its group structure fostered stylistic pluralism and sensitivity to context.

Horselydown Square

Shad Thames, Southwark, London
1986–8, Julyan Wickham and Associates

Horselydown Square demonstrates post-modernism's strengths in urban planning – compact, mixing uses and with elevations that announce a sense of place. Six blocks of ground-floor shops, first-floor offices and upper-floor maisonettes muddle happily around courtyards over a basement car park. Horselydown Square itself drifts into Anchor Court, knitting in older buildings and nestling into an existing street pattern. Austrian architect Camillo Sitte first preached the joys of wandering through the unexpected in the 1880s, something the 1960s townscape movement over-defined and prettified but which Wickham realized here. The density and mixed use help, together with rare public access in this quarter of London. Wickham's collaborator was Michael Baumgarten, a fellow architect who had been part of the artists' community that first settled the area in the 1970s before becoming a developer, in association with Bison Concrete and Berkley House.

The blocks into the courtyard are eight storeys, defined by giant columns for the commercial floors, while narrower pilasters over three storeys of flats give out before reaching the stone-clad top floor and brick penthouses. This balanced chequerboard of blue curved balconies and oriels collapses at the ends into bull-nosed waterfalls of glass and orange render that almost collide. Yet behind the render lurks a massive concrete frame, much of it pre-cast, worthy of any brutalist and designed for speed.

An intended pavilion for the piazza was abandoned in favour of a whimsical fountain. The shop fronts were refurbished in 2017.

Marco Polo House

Queenstown Road, Battersea, London
1987–8, demolished 2014; Ian Pollard

Pollard's prominent office building challenged every conceit that a building should be architect-designed, well detailed and serious. Marco Polo House offered bands of grey and white cladding contrasted with black glass, broken pediments taken from Philip Johnson's AT&T building in New York and elephantine feet to its implied order. The architectural press prevaricated between calling it a liquorice allsort or a giant humbug. There was technical innovation: it was the first use in Europe of neopariès, an expensive opaque glass-like product from Japan; the curtain wall was novel in resting one sheet of glass on another without a metal frame, and plastic security cards doubled as credit cards for use in vending machines and the staff restaurant. And there was architectural form: the pediments denoted a cross-in-square plan inspired by Palladio's Villa Rotonda, within which was a giant atrium. Yet the facade was ungainly and there was no attempt to hide bodges behind it. What palled was that the designer was no architect but a flamboyant developer who called his building 'fun'.

Pollard began training as an architect, but was advised by a tutor that if he really wanted to build as he wanted he should become the client. So he switched to chartered surveying and, aged 26, launched Flaxyard PLC. Here he acted for the British Rail Property Board and the building was squeezed alongside the viaduct into Victoria Station. Viewed from there, the architecture was clearly skin deep.

The building's demolition in 2014 sparked the same questions over the future of post-modernism that had greeted its arrival 28 years earlier.

Homebase

Warwick Road, Royal Borough of Kensington and Chelsea, London 1988–90, demolished 2014; Ian Pollard

Sainsbury's commissioned a flurry of architecturally exciting stores in the late 1980s. Most were determinedly high-tech, but here the company's architectural committee chose the ancient Egyptian style to convey the idea of permanence and to create a landmark. It reported that Pollard's design was 'a bit over the top, but does it matter?'[6] Lord Sainsbury was more wary, insisting on the removal of Corinthian columns and the brightest colours.

Pollard's elevation paid shameless homage to Stirling and Wilford's **Neue Staatsgalerie** in Stuttgart with its green, skirt-like window and stripes of stone and granite. Where the cladding shifted from fine Lepine limestone to render, a carved line resembled that denoting a break on architectural drawings. Out of this stepped a portico with an upswept Egyptian top, and a colonnade of short fat columns with Corinthian capitals. Most exciting was a frieze that mixed pyramids with power tools – a useful update for the God Seth, dubbed 'Ankh and Decker' by Pollard (a pun on 'Black and Decker'), who carefully researched the programme of iconography with the stonemason, Richard Kindersley. The Goddess Neith, Protector of the Dead, traditionally seated, found appropriate relaxation on the plant room door.

Pollard also considered building a pyramid as a leisure centre in Kensington, and was about to build a complex of dance studios, shops and offices, the Peckham Pomp, when in the recession of the early 1990s his property company went bust. He later secured further notoriety with his second wife, Barbara, as UK television's 'Naked Gardeners', revealing himself as an old-fashioned 1960s eccentric.

Italian Centre

John Street, Ingram Street and Cochrane Street, Glasgow
1988–91, Page & Park

In the late 1980s David Page and Brian Park represented a new generation
of architects who embraced Glasgow's Victorian and earlier history.
Their work with Donald Loan and John Sheridan, directors of developers
Classical House, coincided with Glasgow's year as Britain's first City of
Culture (1990) and a reappraisal of what John Betjeman called 'Britain's
greatest Victorian City'.

The Italian Centre is inherently simple. A block of 19th-century
tenements was carefully restored externally, but its insides were scooped
out to create a new courtyard, whose striped stone walls form a plinth
for rendered brickwork and pretty steel balconies and walkways above. A
rill gurgles down the centre of the tight space. The water suggests Italy, as
does the sculpture, particularly that depicting Mercurius and Italia on the
external parapets by Alexander Stoddart. Work in the courtyard by Shona
Kinloch pays homage to Marino Marini, and a metal mural is by Jack Sloan.
Pavement cafés and Italian fashion designers moved in, as did Page and Park
themselves. But the building also commemorates the many thousands of
people of Italian extraction living in Glasgow, most of whom can trace their
origins to large-scale immigration in the 1890s.

The result is infinitely more serious than Charles Moore's Piazza d'Italia
in New Orleans, suggesting a long-term architectural fusion between
new building, conservation and sculpture. In 1991 the Italian Centre won
both Saltire and Civic Trust Awards. Page & Park's later projects were more
thoroughly modern.

Minster Court

Mincing Lane, City of London
1988–93, GMW Partnership

From earliest times, Mincing Lane was a centre of trade; the establishment of sale rooms here in the 19th century prefigures the area's latter-day specialism as London's insurance business district. At the height of 'Big Bang' financial fever, Prudential Assurance developed a linked trio of speculative offices, with open-plan dealer floors on the three lowest storeys. The high-tech interior of No. 3 Minster Court, completed by YRM as the London Underwriting Centre, sits a little incongruously with the slick shock of the façade.

Early exponents of American curtain walling, the commercial practice Gollins Melvin Ward was described by James Stirling as 'the best of the safe, understandable moderns'.[7] GMW's about-turn from their previous Miesian efforts for Sheffield University (1959–65) and Commercial Union/P&O (1963–9) was shocking at the time. But along with the transatlantic post-modernism of No. 54 Lombard Street (1986–94), Minster Court now reads as a rational tracking of developments in American commercial architecture, its neo-Gothic prefigured by Philip Johnson's PPG Place in Pittsburgh (1981–4).

Against the building's clip-on Gothic cladding, slickly executed in pink Brazilian granite by Josef Gartner, is set a theatrical glass entrance court. While the architects professed their admiration for the expressionism of Bruno Taut and Hans Poelzig, more self-evident is Minster Court's affinity with Anton Furst's Gotham City in *Batman* (1989). Unkindly dubbed 'Munster Court', the newly completed pile stood in for the headquarters of Cruella de Vil (played by Glenn Close) in Disney's 1996 remake of *101 Dalmatians*.

Three Brindleyplace

Birmingham
1996–8, Demetri Porphyrios

Brindleyplace is a mixed development by Argent Group PLC, set in an angle of two canals on the site of long-derelict factories where John Chatwin produced a master plan in 1993, in succession to Terry Farrell. The architects for the office buildings were chosen for their skill with brick, with Porphyrios selected alongside modernists Allies & Morrison and Stanton Williams. The buildings share a common red brick and a tripartite division into base, main storeys and attic. Three Brindleyplace is the centrepiece, its seven storeys subsumed into an arcaded rusticated base and a giant attic with a colonnade and gabled ends like a rooftop temple. An Italianate tower was placed where it could be seen from outside the development. Porphyrios's sources are Venetian Renaissance, as revived and revised by Léon and Rob Krier. The ground floor features pointed arches reminiscent of the Doge's Palace in Venice, yet from a springing of Doric columns of reconstituted stone – creative rather than correct. Inside, a Doric order, partly fluted like muscly legs in long socks, leads to an atrium dressed in a giant Corinthian order. It was Porphyrios's first built commission for a major developer.

Porphyrios was born in Greece and, although he studied at Princeton and now teaches at Yale, his work is European in tradition. He typifies architects whose private houses are purely classical but whose commercial works assume a post-modern quality when absorbing more storeys and greater scale. The building was quickly let and Porphyrios was commissioned to build the simpler Seven Brindleyplace in 2003–5.

James
Stirling

Page 106: The corner tower at 1 Poultry, by James Stirling,
Michael Wilford & Associates, 1994–8

bullient, provocative, inventive and bloody-minded, James Stirling
(1926–92) is a towering yet little-understood figure in 20th-century
architecture. In partnership with James Gowan (1923–2015), he
established an international reputation with the Leicester University
Engineering Building (1961–3), but his uncompromising attitude and a
reputation for construction glitches divided opinion in Britain, where
commissions dried up in the recessionary 1970s. 'As anyone will know
who keeps up with the English highbrow weeklies,' Reyner Banham wrote
in 1984, 'the only approvable attitude to James Stirling is one of sustained
execration and open or veiled allegations of incompetence'.[1] Elsewhere it was
different. After the breakthrough of the Stuttgart **Neue Staatsgalerie**, won at
competition in 1977, a series of prestigious projects in Europe and the United
States kick-started a second, largely international career. It is this later period,
distinguished by an urban contextualism and a post-modernist architectural
language, which forms the focus of this chapter.

James Stirling was born in Glasgow, the son of a Scottish ship's engineer
and a Scottish-Irish schoolteacher, and raised in Liverpool. After war service,
he studied at the Liverpool School of Architecture from 1945 to 1950 where he
became fascinated by the city's 19th-century architecture and was influenced
by his final-year tutor, the architectural historian Colin Rowe. Speculative
but brilliant, Rowe's work forged formal connections between Modern
Movement, Renaissance and mannerist architecture. Arriving in London
in 1950, Stirling worked as an assistant for the respected modernist practice
Lyons Israel & Ellis, while teaching at the Regent Street Polytechnic and
making contact with Alison and Peter Smithson, Reyner Banham and others
associated with the Independent Group. Stirling established partnerships
with James Gowan from 1956 to 1963 and with former assistant Michael
Wilford from 1971 until Stirling's death in 1992.

James Stirling with his Thomas Hope chair, photographed by Philip Sayer in 1985

After the split with Gowan, Stirling established a small office at No. 75 Gloucester Place in London. Here he developed a collaborative design process that enabled him to oversee several projects simultaneously. Hand drawing was the medium of communication at every stage, from the development of initial concepts to presentation and supervision of contractors. 'Everything was about the drawings which were worked over and over, with Jim keeping total control', John Corrigan recalled.[2] Stirling himself drew little and had no drawing board or sketchbook but instead filled small scraps of paper or plane tickets with intricate doodles. More often he marked up assistants' drawings, a process known in the office as 'redlining'. Successive rounds of editing and criticism introduced an analytical clarity to the arrangement of parts or the route through the building. The use of thumbnail sketches to design large buildings helps to explain the juxtapositions of scale which characterize Stirling's work.

Stirling's output can be broadly categorized into a number of overlapping phases, each defined by a consistent palette of materials and forms. Le Corbusier was the prevailing influence on both his 1950 thesis and a 1953 competition entry for Sheffield University in which components are packed into a liner-like framework. In the 1950s Stirling developed a brick vocabulary: the unbuilt Forsyth House at Woolton Park of 1954 is a cluster of mono-pitched forms while the Ham Common Flats (1955–8), the job which launched Stirling and Gowan into practice, adopts the brutalist language of Le Corbusier's Maisons Jaoul (1954–5) in the Paris suburb of Neuilly-sur-Seine.

A 1959 competition entry for Selwyn College, Cambridge anticipates the 'red trilogy' of the Leicester University Engineering Building, the Cambridge University History Faculty (1964–8) and the Florey Building for Queen's College, Oxford (1968–71). At Leicester, poised, dynamic masses, constructivist in spirit but owing little to any single source, are sheathed in tiles, engineering bricks and patent glazing. Other projects flirted with the imagery and technique of industrialized building, such as the pre-cast concrete cladding of the Andrew Melville hall of residence at the University of St Andrews (1967–8), the colourful, clip-on glass reinforced polyester (GRP) panels of the Olivetti Training School at Haslemere (1971–2) and the Southgate Estate at Runcorn New Town (1970–7).

In the 1970s Stirling moved towards a more contextual and post-modernist approach based on the European city and its classical architecture. A catalyst in the process was Léon Krier, who worked for Stirling as an unqualified assistant from 1968 to 1970 and again in 1973–4. He was regarded by Stirling as a draftsman, but he nevertheless provided an important bridge to a European architectural culture. Born in Luxembourg, Krier abandoned his studies at the Stuttgart technical university, working instead with his brother Rob on competition designs. He was accepted into the Stirling office on the strength of his beguiling drawings, whose clear-headed,

The Southgate Estate at Runcorn New Town, built between 1970 and 1977 to designs by James Stirling (demolished in 1989)

mono-line style was influenced by Le Corbusier's heroic period and French neoclassicism. Krier's influence on the way in which the practice presented and documented its work is evident in the 1975 volume of Stirling's collected works, sometimes known as the 'black book'.[3] Working with Stirling, he devised a series of up-view or 'worm's eye' axonometric views – a technique invented by the 19th-century architectural historian Auguste Choisy – that were often pared back to show how parts related or how a visitor moved through the building.

Krier also worked on architectural competitions, and his contributions to the Siemens Research Centre in Munich (1969) and Derby Civic Centre (1970) presage contrasting aspects of Stirling's post-modernism. Based on Krier's 1968 competition entry for Bielefeld University, the long, narrow scheme for Siemens is dominated by pairs of monumental cylindrical towers that are bisected by a boulevard of shops and cafés along with corporate amenities. The plan and symmetrical section are that of a megastructure like London's Brunswick Centre but in neoclassical dress; Krier described it as a 'Palladian machine'.[4]

Whereas previous projects were situated at greenfield locations or on the outskirts of towns, the rebuilding of Derby's Market Square confronted the practice with a historic urban setting. The horseshoe-shaped complex acts as the backdrop to a public square in which the façade of the burnt-out assembly hall was retained but inclined at forty degrees. This, a 'Spirit of Ecstasy' statue (the city's biggest employer was Rolls-Royce) and a stepped phalanx of telephone boxes offered a surreal mixture of the everyday and the monumental, behind which a glazed façade was to ascend to a barrel-vaulted galleria based on London's Burlington Arcade.

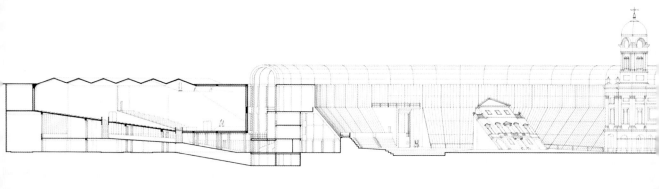

Competition entry for Derby Civic Centre by James Stirling and Léon Krier, 1970

Comparable was the practice's first gallery project, an unbuilt proposal for a tiny arts centre for the University of St Andrews (1971), where curved galleries flank a Georgian house in the manner of Palladio's Villa Badoer. Stirling's move towards an urban contextualism was all the more surprising given the self-containment of the 1959 competition entry for Churchill College, Cambridge or the wilfully anti-townscape stance of the Cambridge History Faculty. An important influence on Stirling was Colin Rowe's *Collage City*, first published in article form in 1975.[5] This text, together with the influence of O M Ungers and Aldo Rossi, provided Stirling with a theoretical framework that permitted juxtaposition and montage as well as spatial and historical continuity.

In 1975, the practice entered two museum competitions in West Germany: the Nordrhein-Westfalen Museum in Düsseldorf and the Wallraf-Richartz Museum in Cologne. They did not win, but their designs contributed to a third competition entry of 1977 that did: the **Neue Staatsgalerie** in Stuttgart. Applying the principles of Derby and the St Andrews Arts Centre to major civic buildings in urban centres, the 'German trio' established the preoccupations of Stirling's later work. Thus their interplay of solid and void, assembly of elemental forms, reuse of historic fragments and classical-cum-modernist vocabulary can be traced through to the **Berlin Social Science Centre** (1984–7), the Center for the Performing Arts at Cornell University (1986–8) and the posthumous Stuttgart **Music School and Theatre Academy** (1993–4) and **1 Poultry** in the City of London (1994–8).

For Stirling, the passing of what Reyner Banham called 'the age of the masters' brought a loss of certainty yet also a sense of liberation that helped to overcome a creative impasse or suppression. The moment was celebrated in Stirling's contribution to the 1978 Roma Interrotta exhibition, in which a dozen architects were invited to submit their interpretation of sections of the 1748 Nolli plan of Rome. Stirling incorporated 30 built and unbuilt works into the fabric of the city, as if he was seeking to revalidate his collected works as an urban statement.

Stirling was a magpie with an eye for detail, an unbounded appetite for architectural history, and a seemingly photographic memory. In the earlier works, ostensibly grounded in modernism, he could not suppress veiled or abstracted allusions to village housing (the scheme presented at the 1956 Congrès internationaux d'architecture modern); Victorian warehouses and factories (the housing at Avenham, Preston of 1959–61); the glass lantern roofs of 19th-century public libraries (Cambridge History Faculty) and the Milanese 'Liberty style' (Perrygrove sheltered housing at Blackheath, completed in 1964).

Stirling regarded post-modernism with a mixture of ambivalence and guarded curiosity – Wilford recalls him returning from teaching at Yale with the 'great find' of a copy of Venturi's *Complexity and Contradiction*:

> I feel on the fringe of post-modern but I've always felt on the fringe [Stirling said in 1986]. I never felt that I was brutalist and I don't feel now that I am a post-modernist. I'm curious about post-modernism and I'm interested, in a way, but I don't feel part of it.[6]

Although he admired architects then working within the post-modern canon such as Robert Venturi, Michael Graves and Arata Isozaki, Stirling was reluctant to be confined into any stylistic pigeonhole and disparaging of what he felt was the superficial historicism of the style. Yet like his mentor Colin Rowe, much of his work was preoccupied with the relationship between Modern Movement principles and historical continuity. Looking back over three decades of work in 1981, Stirling remarked that all his work oscillated between modernist abstraction and representational aspects such as tradition, vernacular and history.[7] His later works demonstrate the hybrid character of post-modernism, counterbalancing explicitly representational and abstract elements in the same building.

Neue Staatsgalerie

Stuttgart, Germany
1979–83, James Stirling, Michael Wilford & Associates

The Neue Staatsgalerie is Stirling's late masterpiece. It was one of a trio of competition entries for German museums, preceded by 1975 schemes for Düsseldorf and Cologne. The design was commenced in 1977 as Stirling departed to teach at Yale; he put a small group onto the project, suggesting a development of the Düsseldorf design. Thus aspects of the earlier scheme formed a starting point for Stuttgart: an entrance forecourt raised above car parking, galleries ranged around a circular sculpture court and a vocabulary of coursed ashlar contrasted with a rippling glass entrance hall.

The Stuttgart site steeply falls down to the autobahn-like Konrad Adenauer Straße; to the north is the neoclassical Staatsgalerie of 1843 (in fact a post-war reconstruction). Like Schinkel's Altes Museum in Berlin, an enfilade of galleries encloses an open-air rotunda, giving rise to a plan that echoes the original Staatsgalerie. Stirling set back this building from the busy boulevard, devising an entrance sequence through a terraced landscape. The brief required that a public footpath be provided through the site without entering the building. This takes the form of an architectural promenade that criss-crosses the axial plan, traversing ramps and winding around the rotunda to arrive at an upper sculpture terrace.

Stirling observed of his design that for every act there is a counter act, and indeed it can be read as a series of polarities: representational–abstract; monumental–informal; solid–void; tradition–transgression. Another is antique–modern: classical forms and finely wrought ashlar commingle with brightly coloured modernist references. The latter – including the fat pink and blue rails, the constructivist zig-zag canopy, the undulating curtain wall and the apple-green Pirelli rubber flooring of the entrance hall – serve to guide visitors along the route. Mannerist jokes, including the 'ruined' retaining wall or the Doric order that rises from the floor of the courtyard like a Wurlitzer organ, express the ambivalent status of the late-20th century cultural institution as a place of distraction and amusement as well as a temple to art.

To the south, the pedestrian walkway continues via a segmental vault through the projecting chamber theatre. This L-plan building uses the Staatsgalerie's coursed ashlar as a stone base, with rendered upper floors punctuated by small square windows in the manner of Aldo Rossi. A decade later the building was joined by its symmetrical counterpart, in the form of the Music School and Theatre Academy, forming another three-sided courtyard. The most prominent element of this phase (designed from 1987 but constructed after Stirling's death) is the cylindrical tower of the Music School that contrasts with the circular void of the Staatsgalerie. This the architects likened to the cork out of the bottle.

Arthur M. Sackler Museum

Harvard University, 485 Broadway, Cambridge,
Massachusetts, United States
1982–5, James Stirling, Michael Wilford & Associates

In *Big Jim*, his biography of James Stirling, Mark Girouard describes Harvard's Sackler Museum as 'a typical Jim story: comic and tragic, mixed success and failure, not enough money, too many rows'.[8] The result is an intriguingly imperfect building arising from a mix of promise and compromise. In 1979, Seymour Slive, director of the Fogg Museum, commissioned Stirling to design an extension on a new site across the road, rehousing the ancient, oriental and Islamic collections and adding staff offices and teaching facilities.

Stirling devised an L-shaped building that occupies the whole of the tight site. A lofty entry hall gives way to a tall, narrow staircase that rises through the building to divide rear galleries from front offices. Coloured in bands of purple and buff plaster, it is top lit with roof lights, while internal windows bring borrowed light from the adjacent corridors. Stirling contrived a disordered street elevation by centring the windows on rooms of varying dimensions. The fenestration pattern is ordered by window-height stripes of buff and grey bricks (although green and pink was his first choice).

The *pièce de resistance*, an enclosed footbridge across Broadway to the Fogg, was thwarted after local objections. Instead, pylon-like columns flank a cleft-like entrance, which to Stirling suggested a visage looking out over the campus with an 'Eastern or antique gaze'.[9] With the opening of a new facility by Renzo Piano in 2014, Harvard's three art museums were brought under a single roof. The Sackler now houses the Department of History of Art and Architecture.

Clore Gallery

Tate Britain, Millbank, London
Designed 1980–1, built 1982–7, James Stirling,
Michael Wilford & Associates

The architects were appointed in 1979 to plan the expansion of the Tate
Gallery (now Tate Britain), reusing the former hospital alongside.
A bicentennial exhibition of the work of J M W Turner in 1974–5 had
prompted calls to honour his will, in which he had bequeathed his paintings
to the nation on condition that a gallery be built for them. Vivian Duffield
offered sponsorship in December 1979, and proposals for the hospital were
shelved in favour of a new gallery to be named after her father, the developer
Charles Clore.

Stirling's scheme develops his slightly earlier gallery at Harvard in
being L-shaped and dominated by a staircase, but here it doubles back. The
new galleries share a common level with those in Sidney Smith's original
building of 1893–7, and Stirling continues Smith's cornice, punching through
windows in the return wing. The hospital lodge had also to be retained. The
façade is clearly a cladding, with a grid of Portland stone infilled with render
near the main Tate building and brick towards the lodge. To fit in a ground-
floor lecture theatre and reading room, the entrance is low, set in a sunken
courtyard and denoted by the only continuous stone walling, which Stirling
then pierced with a triangular opening. The geometry of the entrance and the
gridded façade are reminiscent of Gunnar Asplund's Lister and Gothenburg
court houses respectively. The green windows repeat those at Stuttgart, but
here with square panes. Inside, the staircase handrail is pink, as at Leicester
Engineering Building, and the gallery entrance is sapphire and ultramarine
blue – a contrast to the more respectful galleries.

Berlin Social Science Centre (WZB)

Tiergarten, Berlin, Germany
1984–7, James Stirling, Michael Wilford & Associates

This project for a research institute in the social sciences was won at limited competition in 1979. Five building types – amphitheatre, keep, basilica, campanile and stoa – each identifying a different department, along with a protected Beaux-Arts building (of 1891–4 by August Busse), are juxtaposed around an irregular court. Stirling 'came into the office fresh from a holiday at Barfleur, brandishing a little book on the different architectural styles and saying "We'll have one of each"'.[10] Only the keep was not built; its outline is instead marked by a topiary garden.

A collage of building types technique was felt appropriate for a district replanned after wartime destruction with free-standing buildings such as Mies van der Rohe's National Gallery and Hans Scharoun's Philharmonic Hall. The plan can be compared with Louis Kahn's project for the Dominican Motherhouse in Media, Pennsylvania (1965–8) and O M Unger's 1964 proposal for student housing at the University of Twente in Enschede, in the Netherlands.

The exteriors are equally uninhibited, and were likened by one assistant to striped pyjamas and known to some Berliners as the wedding cake. Bands of light blue and pink render on a limestone plinth unite the assorted forms, the palette influenced by neoclassical Helsinki and St Petersburg. The plasterers were encouraged to abandon their perfection for a 'handmade' finish. Chunky sandstone frames project from the windows, suggesting the security of a thick-walled church or fortress.

Electa Bookshop

Biennale Giardini, Venice
1991, James Stirling, Michael Wilford & Associates

In 1989, Stirling was invited by his friend Francesco Dal Co to design a little
bookshop to mark the 1991 Venice Architecture Biennale. It was to be located
in the Biennale Giardini, a collection of national pavilions among trees,
east of the Arsenale. Stirling initially conceived a baptistery-like octagonal
building at the intersection of the principal boulevards, but as he could not
face removing a single tree he opted instead for a long, narrow form aligned
with the main route and squeezed between rows of trees, which appear like
the columns along a loggia. Their removal in recent years changes the way in
which the building is encountered.

Drawing upon the watery setting, Stirling with Thomas Muirhead
devised a 'bookship–boatshop', about the size of a *vaporetto*, with a curved
prow and a 45-degree patinated copper roof like an upturned hull, or perhaps
like the thatched roof of a *cason*, a sort of vernacular lodge found in the
Venetian lagoon. Stirling, who related that he was conceived on board a cargo
ship moored at New York harbour, felt that 'the closer modern architecture
gets to water and boats, the more amusing it becomes'.[11] Rejecting a
centralized entrance, he decided that the vessel should be entered on the long
axis, marked by a white-rendered gable end and a funnel-cum-illuminated
sign. The broadly oversailing roof is raised towards the apex so that, as
Muirhead explained, 'the bright clear light of a Venetian summer, filtering
down through the overhanging branches [throws] the shadows of dancing
leaves onto the pages of an open book'.[12]

1 Poultry

Bank, City of London
Designed 1986–8, built 1994–8; listed Grade II* in 2016;
James Stirling, Michael Wilford & Associates

1 Poultry is James Stirling's definitive late work in England. His commission
came from Lord Palumbo in July 1985 after an earlier scheme designed by
Mies van der Rohe was rejected at public inquiry. Palumbo's development
spurred a conservation battle over the fate of several listed buildings, not least
John Belcher's Mappin & Webb building (1870–1). While various architects,
including Stirling and Terry Farrell, prepared schemes incorporating it,
following a second public inquiry its replacement was eventually approved.

If Stirling could countenance the loss of Belcher's Gothic Revival set-
piece, he nevertheless venerated its City site, describing it as 'this spider's
web intersection surrounded by all those heroes' – the heroes in question
included George Dance's Mansion House, Lutyens's Midland Bank, Cooper's
National Westminster Bank and Soane's Bank of England.[13] For a speculative
development Palumbo's brief was unusually elaborate and civic-minded,
combining offices, shops, a pub, access to Bank underground station and a
rooftop restaurant, punningly named Coq d'Argent.

1 Poultry is a thin triangle pinned to the ground by a huge drum. The
alternating bands of buff and red sandstone are as striped as a Butterfield
church. Over a double-height colonnade and a giant torus moulding, bow-
fronted stone bays alternate with angled glass. This geometric shuffle reprises
Stirling's 1978 scheme for New York townhouses, while the stubby mushroom
column of the Green Man pub on Queen Victoria Street (picked out in
bright yellow with typical Stirling perversity) is a borrowing from the **Neue
Staatsgalerie**. Into the Poultry elevation is set a terracotta frieze of 1875 by
Joseph Kramer, re-sited from the demolished 12–13 Poultry.

Bucklersbury Passage bisects the complex and from the central open-
air court one can access a lower concourse level with retail units and
connections into Bank station or by lift to the rooftop restaurant. This
great drum is interpenetrated by a triangle of offices, clad in indigo faience

tiles with window reveals in signature pink, yellow and cyan. The layered geometries recall Stirling's respect for Louis Kahn's architecture, particularly his Adath Jeshurun Synagogue project and the diagrid vaults of the Yale University Art Gallery.

The apex is another set piece. A turret with inset clock and cantilevered viewing platforms rises over a round-headed entrance and a glass prow. Apart from the Mappin & Webb building, Stirling's tower suggests such diverse sources as Roman rostral columns, submarine conning towers and a 1974 scheme for a Tuscan tower house by his former assistant, Léon Krier.

1 Poultry's dynamic play of geometries and the references to Stirling's other works and those of his heroes makes it an inventive and gregarious companion to the likes of Lutyens' bank. 'Common to both buildings', Colin St John Wilson remarked, 'are an element of wit, of knowingness, of "the high game" and it is as if this note is passed from generation to generation.'[14]

Terry Farrell

Page 130: Limehouse studios at West India Docks on the Isle of Dogs, by the Terry Farrell Partnership, 1982–3 (demolished in 1989)

Terry Farrell's post-modern period – like the premiership of Margaret Thatcher – happens to bookend the 1980s. While this no doubt has assisted those reaching for easy pigeonholes, it has also hindered serious reassessment of his work. The path that Farrell took during this decade consistently wrong-footed commentators, as he appeared to lurch from high-tech to post-modernism, from community-based rehabilitation projects to developer clients, and from London sites to opening offices in Edinburgh and Hong Kong. Yet if Farrell's career is assessed as a whole one sees a continuity of approach that runs right through. He worked from 1965 to 1980 in partnership with Nicholas Grimshaw, perhaps the most consistent of all the high-tech architects, and in contrast Farrell has emphasized instead the consistencies that underlie his adaptation to very different conditions and circumstances:

> Many who appear to be working exclusively in one particular idiom
> do so because their palette has not changed, when actually they have
> radically changed their principles. By contrast I have changed the
> palette, the materials, and the kind of programmes ... but my principles
> have remained the same.[1]

The tension between superficial change and inner consistency is a recurrent motif in Farrell's thinking. Reflecting on the connections between styles of dress and architectural fabric, he remarks that while some designers modify their attire over the years while locking themselves into an unchanging architectural idiom, others – notably James Stirling – fixed their sartorial 'look' but continually evolved their architectural appearance. Elsewhere he observed that following the breakup in 1980 of the Farrell/Grimshaw Partnership, it was the latter who changed his address but kept his style.

Terry Farrell at Embankment Place, photographed by Philip Sayer, c.1990

Farrell, however, stayed put, transforming the office interior from Herman Miller Action Office to post-modern oasis.[2]

Farrell was born in 1938 to a 'first-generation respectable' working-class Catholic family of Irish origins, growing up in Sale, Greater Manchester, and Newcastle.[3] In the semi-autobiographical *Place*, he relates how through solitary childhood pursuits (comics, Disney movies, model-making, keeping tropical fish and painting), he escaped into an interior world of invention and colour, developing a sense of independence whilst identifying with 'outsiders, nonconformists and underdogs'.[4] From 1956 to 1961 Farrell studied at the Newcastle University School of Architecture, and in the library discovered the work of Gunnar Asplund, Arne Jacobsen, Richard Neutra, Craig Ellwood, Buckminster Fuller and Frank Lloyd Wright; these were architects of individuality and independence who stood outside the mainstream of the Modern Movement.

Farrell spent his year out in the architect's department of the London County Council, where he designed the sculptural ventilation towers for the Blackwall Tunnel (now listed grade II). In 1962 he travelled to the United States on a Harkness Fellowship, studying at the University of Pennsylvania under Louis Kahn, Denise Scott Brown and Robert Venturi, while Paul Davidoff and Ian McHarg opened his eyes to the civil rights and ecological movements. After a stint working for the planner Colin Buchanan, Farrell in 1965 set up in practice with Grimshaw, an Architectural Association (AA) student who had occupied the adjacent drawing board at County Hall.

With their first project, the conversion of six Bayswater houses into a students' hostel, the dynamics of a 15-year partnership were established.

Clifton Nurseries at Covent Garden, by the Terry Farrell Partnership, 1980-1 (demolished 1988)

Although Farrell planned the flats, organized the services and designed a mobile furniture unit, the focus of press coverage was Grimshaw's self-contained service pod. A pattern of specialisms emerged: Grimshaw's flexible and colourful sheds were hailed as home-grown pioneers of the high-tech movement, whereas Farrell's portfolio was more diverse, if less photogenic, and embraced interiors, social housing and mixed-use projects such as the Colonnades (1974–6). In 1976, they were invited by Charles Jencks to lecture at the AA. Jencks's early writings on post-modernism and the opportunity to collaborate on the design of his **Thematic House** in Lansdowne Walk were both catalysts for Farrell's architectural reinvention.

Farrell's development was equally spurred by disenchantment with the direction of high-tech, which he felt was becoming commoditized into a branch of product design or a businessman's architecture. The divergence within the partnership and its eventual dissolution in May 1980 mirrored the wider fragmentation and crisis of British architecture. Yet Farrell did not turn his back on technology, and his journey towards post-modernism was less a Damascene conversion than a gradual metamorphosis. His post-modern phase is signposted by several earlier projects.

Varied, colourful timber-frame housing for the Maunsel Housing Society in London (1974–81) and the Oakwood housing at Warrington New Town (1978–81) were attempts to reconcile personal taste and local context with mass production. The latter overlapped with 'Learning from Chigwell', a study of residents' adaptations and taste cultures that Farrell initiated when teaching at the AA. Then there were the successive transformations of the suburban house in Maida Vale into which Farrell and his family moved in 1974. With his wife Sue, he created an intricate treasure chest of furniture, patterned fabrics and collectables that reminded him of Alberti's aphorism, 'The city is like a great house, and the house in its turn a small city'.[5] For John Scott, a patron of Farrell/Grimshaw's co-ownership housing at Park Road and much later of CZWG's **Westbourne Grove Public Conveniences**, Farrell helped to convert a pair of houses to make a suitably eclectic setting for his collection of antiques.

The first projects published in Farrell's own name were a series of lightweight temporary pavilions that afforded the opportunity to explore new territory quickly and instinctively. Through Jencks and his wife Maggie Keswick he met Jacob Rothschild, for whom he designed the Clifton Nurseries in Bayswater (1979–80), a greenhouse of double-walled polycarbonate sheeting punctuated by cut-outs of the building in the manner of Robert Venturi. A second garden centre (1980–1) responded to its Covent Garden site with a temple screen front, double the width of the Teflon-coated structure behind and aligned with the axis of King Street. After the Victorian Alexandra Palace in north London was gutted by fire in 1980, Farrell designed a large, two-tone tent for temporary exhibitions, collaborating with Peter Rice and Ian Ritchie on its translucent, PVC-coated skin. Finally, a central London gallery for the Crafts Council (1980–1) was an exercise in three-dimensional layering, set off by blue neon signage.

These low-budget pavilions, coupling retro-Edwardian festivity with high-tech skins, were designed alongside the **Thames Water Authority Operations Centre** in Reading. They 'took High-Tech out to play' in Deyan Sudjic's phrase, reconciling building technology with popular taste cultures.[6] Combining the 'double coding' advocated by Jencks with American-inspired billboards and Art Deco, **TV-am** and the short-lived television studios at Limehouse Basin (1982–3) are perhaps Farrell's most uninhibited and joyful works. They mark a cathartic moment in his career: 'I suppose everything

I had suppressed professionally and emotionally tended to burst out in my buildings', he recalled.[7] The publicity value reaped by the TV-am eggcups and the garden centres was out of all proportion to their size and budget, and for the first and only time in his career Farrell found himself in fashion.

Like his heroes Buckminster Fuller and Otto Wagner, Farrell found his voice fairly late in life. A series of commercial commissions provided an entrée to the City of London and saw Farrell's post-modernism morph into a bankers' classicism. The Allied Irish Bank on Queen Street (*c.* 1984–5) and Midland Bank, Fenchurch Street (1986–7) are tripartite compositions detailed in thin slivers of polished and flamed granite, the former quoting the bolt-on cladding of Wagner's Austrian Postal Savings Bank in Vienna. But the best illustration of Farrell's contextualism was his sensitive yet bold rehabilitation of historic buildings, including Tobacco Dock (1985–90) and Hatton Street Studios (1985–8, to house Farrell's practice), while the patch and mend strategy of **Comyn Ching** influenced his 1984–7 proposals for the 1 Poultry site and pointed the way to his future development.

Farrell's output at the end of the decade was dominated by three major commissions. **Embankment Place**, **Alban Gate** and the first of a number of proposals for Moor House in London Wall (1986) pile formal elements

Allied Irish Bank, 36 Queen Street, City of London, by the Terry Farrell Partnership, c.1984–5 (refaced 2013)

Comyn Ching, remodelling and new corner buildings by Terry Farrell, designed from 1976 and built in 1983-7.

derived from the work of Michael Graves into monumental assemblages that command their urban su rroundings. The sis Building is Farrell's last work wholly in the post-modern idiom; later projects, such as the Edinburgh International Conference Centre (1993–5) and the Peak Tower in Hong Kong (1993–7), modulate into an expressive modernism deriving its visual effect from engineering and bold geometries.

Farrell, like his modernist peers, has tended to downplay talk of styles, vocabularies and influences, preferring to dwell on the larger concerns of urban design. Indeed, as is apparent from the projects profiled in this chapter, the connections of his buildings to their urban context and his work as an architect–planner became increasingly relevant and ambitious throughout the 1980s. The master plans for the South Bank (1984–92), King's Cross (1987) and Paternoster Square (1989–92), although influenced by Léon Krier's contemporary proposals, nevertheless made thoughtful contributions to the ongoing debate on the planning of London. They were followed by mixed-use proposals for Edinburgh (1989–92), Birmingham (1990–2), Newcastle (1991–2) and Leeds (1989–92) as well as overseas projects. The urban design work is approached with the same values – thrifty pragmatism, inclusivity and historic continuity – that characterize Farrell's architecture.

TV-am studios

Hawley Crescent, Camden, London
1981–3, Terry Farrell Partnership

Farrell's headquarters for TV-am, the UK's first breakfast television franchise, was a post-modern landmark for the media age. Working within the constraints of a design-and-build contract, a fast-track programme and a tight budget, Farrell transformed an industrial premises with wit and imagination, so creating an instant brand for the fledgling media corporation. Like his contemporary Limehouse Studios, TV-am was a significant yet ultimately ephemeral building. Only a few months after the station went on air, a management takeover resulted in internal alterations, while the supercharged street front outlasted the TV-am franchise only to be reclad in 2012–13.

Farrell was invited by TV-am director of programmes Michael Deakin to submit a proposal for the refurbishment of the Ewart Studios in Wandsworth. When this site fell through, Camden Council planners suggested the former Henlys Rover dealership, whose site lay between the scruffy Hawley Crescent and the Regent's Canal. Farrell initially proposed a symmetrical sunburst that would pierce the building's flat roof with four skylight strips radiating from a circular entrance court. The engineer Peter Rice later devised a Teflon-coated fabric sun to hang over the court. When this proved unaffordable, Farrell instead remodelled the existing structures, focusing on the front and back façades and the creation of an atrium from an irregularly shaped void. Each portion was delegated to a different team, working independently and in friendly competition.

The full-height atrium became the social heart of the station. A 'global village' narrative was elaborated across its east–west axis, including a Japanese pavilion, Mesopotamian ziggurat staircase, Italian garden and Midwestern gulch. The package-tour iconography shares the literalism of Hans Hollein's Austrian Travel Agency in Vienna (1978–9), although the stage-set detailing is closer to the Strada Novissima at the 1980 Venice Architecture Biennale. The bland décor of the sets was incongruent.

On Hawley Crescent, the studios and entrance court were screened by a sinuous, billboard-like façade. A pop rustication was created with diminishing courses of profiled steel separated by roll mouldings in TV-am colours, with the whole raised on a stepped and tiled podium. Supergraphic quoins, extruded from the station's initials by the art director Doug Maxwell, announced the building's presence to Camden High Street and Kentish Town Road. A giant openwork arch – a Meccano model of Vanbrugh's bridge at Blenheim – provided the sunburst motif that Farrell sought.

A canal-side presence was justified by TV-am's hospitality boat, on a permanent mooring. New arched windows, based on the adjacent Camden Brewery, were let into the rear shed, while its saw-tooth roof was crowned with a dozen fibreglass eggcups. The £1,200 cost of the breakfast eggs was borne by Farrell's practice but the station reaped their publicity benefit. TV-am heralds the media age with a lively montage of sources and techniques, including American Deco, Chelsea's Michelin House, residual high-tech, the 'decorated sheds' of Robert Venturi and London's industrial vernacular.

Thames Water Authority Operations Centre

Rose Kiln Lane, Fobney, Reading
1981–2, Terry Farrell Partnership

Farrell's operations centre for Thames Water Authority (TWA) is a transitional work: a manifesto for a pluralistic, contradictory and hybridized high-tech. Also straddling the breakup of the Farrell Grimshaw Partnership, it is intriguing to imagine what Nick Grimshaw made of the design.

TWA requested a combination of a visitor centre and operations headquarters for its sewage treatment works near Reading. Farrell's symmetrical H-plan (as in H_2O) segregates guests and operatives by locating the former along the crossbar separating two parallel operations wings. Approaching ceremonially along the axis, visitors are treated to a wave of curved glass cascading from a first-floor gallery over the double-height visitor centre. The tunnel-vaulted viewing gallery terminates in giant porthole windows that peep over the eaves line (likened by the architect to bubbles or frogs' eyes). TWA translates into glass the curved extrusions of Farrell's Bayswater Clifton Nurseries and Alexandra Pavilion, the resultant form recalling César Pelli's Pacific Design Center (1971–5).

TWA seems designed for colour photography. Its gridded skin is tinted blue and the windows give airbrush-like reflections of the sky. Inside, hazy blues and pinks combine with reflective surfaces and exposed structure. It shares with **tv-am** a graphic quality: the ubiquitous circle motifs, and the rising and falling waves of the door handles and seating echo the TWA logo. Like John Outram's **Isle of Dogs Pumping Station** this industrial building is suffused with elemental symbolism: earth (the perimeter berm), water (glass cascade) and air (sky blue wall).

Comyn Ching

Seven Dials, Covent Garden, London
1983–7, Terry Farrell Partnership; listed Grade II in 2016

The Comyn Ching triangle radiates from Seven Dials in Covent Garden, laid out in 1692 by Sir Thomas Neale after the French Baroque manner of a *rond-point*. Covent Garden had been saved from redevelopment in the 1970s through community action and the listing of over 200 buildings; Comyn Ching marked a milestone in its conservation-led renewal. Since establishing premises in Shelton Street in 1723, the architectural ironmongers Comyn Ching gradually acquired the remaining buildings in the triangle for their workshops and stores. Weighing up their options, they commissioned a master plan from Farrell. As early as 1976 he came up with his solution: three new corner buildings whose sale could fund the restoration of the 26 listed buildings on the site. At the centre, a warren of extensions and outbuildings was scooped out to create a semi-public courtyard, Ching Court.

New entranceways give access to the courtyard, their mannerist detailing derived from the restored shopfronts, while bold doorcases were added to individual properties. The contextual yet robust corner pivots, each one distinct but relating to the next, makes a conscious break with the self-effacing conservation of the listed buildings. The apex, at Seven Dials, is treated as a hinge, with a cylindrical pin rising from stepped flanks of banded brickwork. The layered, pluralist assemblage of Comyn Ching relates to Colin Rowe's *Collage City* (1978) and to Farrell's later proposals for the **1 Poultry** site and Tobacco Dock. By stitching new, mixed-use elements into the historic urban fabric, Comyn Ching is an exemplar of post-modern placemaking at its most intricate.

Henley Royal Regatta Headquarters

Henley-on-Thames, Oxfordshire
1984–6, Terry Farrell Partnership

Few buildings are entirely devoted to an annual sporting fixture, but the Henley Royal Regatta is one such example. Farrell's temple-cum-boatshed, on a fine site beside Henley's 18th-century bridge, perfectly captures the event's singular combination of festivity and propriety. The brief was straightforward: a wet dock at river level for storing the booms and pontoons used to mark out the racecourse; at road level, office accommodation, to include a double-height committee room that opened out onto a riverside balcony. A flat for the club secretary occupies the pediment.

Drawing upon Otto Wagner's Schützenhaus (locks building) on the Danube Canal, as well as Italian suburban villas and Thameside boathouses, Farrell devised a rendered temple front that emerges from a rusticated red brick retaining wall. Stylistically, the design steers closer to the English classical revival than any other Farrell project. The ironic or vulgar symbolism of TV-am is absent, the crossed-oar balconettes and wavy architrave being the only traces of whimsy. Cobalt blue and scarlet and a rear Diocletian window establish a Roman air, yet the slate roof and fidgety brick patterning are English in derivation and Farrell has compared the colour scheme to 'peacocked males in bright club and school blazers and ties'.[8]

The practice was later invited back to Henley to design a balcony and staircase for Fawley Temple, James Wyatt's 1771 eyecatcher on Temple Island, at the start of the course.

Embankment Place

Charing Cross, City of Westminster, London
1987–90, Terry Farrell Partnership

Embankment Place was Farrell's breakthrough. A 'groundscraper' development atop Charing Cross Station, it was the most prominent of a wave of air rights projects that conjured office space over London's rail termini. Air rights required creative structural thinking in relation to the existing station infrastructure. In the negotiations between the developer (Geoffrey Wilson's Greycoat), the site freeholder British Rail and the City of Westminster planners, the commercial component was balanced by a package of public realm improvements. If anyone could interweave public and private spaces, old and new fabric, pedestrians, trains and cars into a single architectural composition, it was Farrell.

Early discussions with planners led to a tiered profile stepping down to the Thames, as at Farrell's 1982 Vauxhall Cross proposals. Ove Arup & Partners, the structural engineers, suggested slinging the office floors from steel tied arches. Their transfer structure minimized the number of columns penetrating the platform and brick vaults below. It found architectural expression in a barrel roof echoing the original station roof and the 'egg in a box' form of the Royal Festival Hall across the river. The office floors were freed up by relocating the four service risers to the perimeter, creating buttress-like forms that rise to a modelled silhouette.

The offices are entered from a five-storey 'foothill' block on the narrow Villiers Street, broken down into contrasting black granite and red brick forms. An upper-level walkway threads behind, linking the railway concourse with the Hungerford Footbridge. Smaller-scale enterprises such as the relocated Players' Theatre were hosted in the tunnel-vaulted Craven Passage.

149

Alban Gate

125 London Wall, City of London
1988-92, Terry Farrell Partnership

Alban Gate takes the air rights concept of **Embankment Place** one step
further: two linked office towers straddle a busy dual carriageway. Its site, at
the junction of London Wall and Wood Street, lies beside the buried Roman
and medieval gateways at Cripplegate, furnishing the model of an inhabited
gatehouse. The intervention meant engaging with the modernist legacy of
London Wall, re-planned in the 1950s with segregated pedestrian access and
rows of matchbox offices. Farrell set his towers at 60 degrees to address both
road axes and devised a four-way circulation system with a pedestrian route
bridging the junction. Alban Gate is thus a literal statement of position in
relation to the Modern Movement.

Joined at the hip, the two blocks are hinged around a common service
core while, in place of a central atrium, giant bow windows bring light deep
into the floorplates. Although the design was slimmed and trimmed at the
planning stage to reduce bulk and modelling, the tri-partite composition
remains liveliest at the base, where there is most activity. Four solid corners,
echoing the turrets of medieval Cripplegate, flank a highly glazed cleft.
Stubbier siblings of Michael Graves's Humana Building in Louisville,
Kentucky, the façades juggle post-modern classical motifs in pastel stripes
of pink and grey granite. The steelwork of Ove Arup & Partners' transfer
structure lends drama to the semi-enclosed walkway.

Monkwell Square to the west was redeveloped as a four-storey residential
block, the City's first housing development since the Barbican to the north.
Designed in a domesticizing idiom of orange-red brick with cast stone
dressings, the block shelters a formal parterre.

SIS Building

85 Albert Embankment, London
1990–4, Terry Farrell & Co

Margaret Thatcher's 1988 approval of a new headquarters for the Secret Intelligence Service (better known as MI6) was the final act in a planning saga that lasted over a decade. Farrell had prepared several schemes for this brownfield site to the south-east of Vauxhall Bridge, beginning with a 1982 competition entry for a larger site. This projected a series of tiered pavilions to maximize daylight and river views. When the developer–sponsor went bust, the downriver portion was bought up by Regalian Properties, for whom Farrell revised his scheme to a residential brief. Then, in 1987, Regalian approached the Property Services Agency with a proposal for a governmental complex. A detailed design incorporating security modifications was hurriedly prepared for planning permission and sale.

There is a pointed contrast between the permeable, mixed-use urban village of the 1982 scheme and SIS's monocultural palace-cum-fortress. Farrell glossed over the differences, stressing communalities in physical form over differences in land-use. Like the earlier schemes (and, on a smaller scale, Limehouse Studios), SIS is a stacked-up, stepped-back ziggurat. Three long blocks descend with relentless symmetry from a cliff-like entrance front, and linking atria and terraces form a portcullis-like plan. Receding planes of green blast-proof curtain walling and cream pre-cast concrete set up a rhythm of solid and void. The massing and stripped detailing suggest various sources from the first half of the 20th century: Giles Gilbert Scott's Bankside and Battersea power stations, the Gotham renderings of Hugh Ferriss and Frank Lloyd Wright's Mayan Revival houses. SIS's move into their conspicuous new headquarters (soon nicknamed Babylon-on-Thames) coincided with a new policy of increased openness as their operations were placed on a statutory footing.

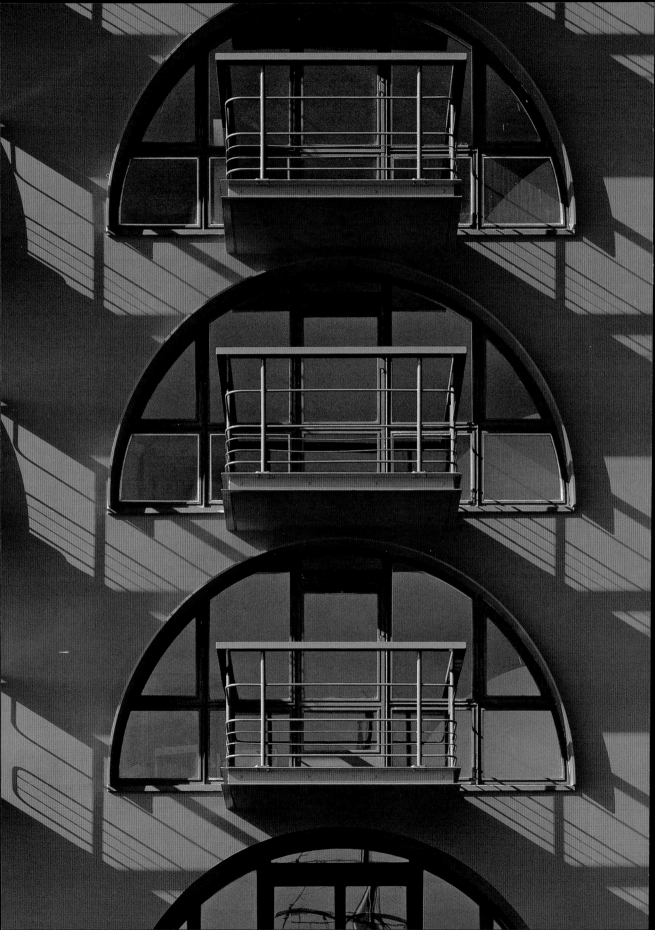

CZWG

Nicholas Campbell (1947–), Roger Zogolovitch (1947–), Rex Wilkinson (1947–) and Piers Gough (1946–) studied together at the Architectural Association (AA) between 1965 and 1971. Their subsequent development was shaped by the preoccupations and reactions of the 1960s: they are the students that never grew up. Their fifth-year tutor, Peter Cook (the leading light of the Archigram group) identified them as a 'mod lot' whose student work was an extension of their personal style and tribal identity:

> As a group they were unmistakable. The rest of the school was in the midst of a technocratic cool, but here were poppy, arty, and in a way *uncool* people, who didn't need an architectural culture to absorb. Their own thing at that moment was infinitely stronger and much more attractive. It belonged to the outside.[1]

Gough's projects conjured cartoonish landscapes populated by cars, fairground-like structures and pleasure-giving technology and delineated with flowing, confident lines. His perspectives identified with American Pop Art yet, like the contemporary, radical-pastoral phase of Archigram, are recognizably English. Permissive, individualist and unapologetically consumerist, their AA years contained all the seeds of the mature CZWG style. A 'pop architecture' sensibility runs unbroken from Gough's student projects, which were contemporary with Robert Venturi and Denise Scott Brown's courses for Yale and UCLA and published in 1972 as *Learning from Las Vegas*.

Impatience to build and an entrepreneurial spirit marked the foursome out from their contemporaries. From their third year, Wilkinson, Zogolovitch and Gough ran a partnership from the AA studio based on family connections with the rag trade. A series of ephemeral boutiques reflected fashionable tastes in retro Art Deco and Edwardiana filtered through a

CZWG in 1986, photographed by Anita Corbin. Clockwise from left: Nicholas Campbell, Roger Zogolovitch, Rex Wilkinson and Piers Gough

shopfitters' vernacular of chrome, mirrors and paint. Knitwit, on South Molton Street, featured ziggurats of sand-coloured tiles, GRP palm tree lamps and changing rooms of quilted brown velvet. It survived long enough to be captured in the pages of the Italian design bible *Domus*.[2]

CZWG's countercultural stance is the essence of their post-modernism. 'To get away from what you see as the faults of the previous generation, it is necessary to jump way over the other side and always slightly too far', Gough has recognized.[3] Reacting against the earnest, reformist wing of modernism (then represented by the Smithsons and the Team Ten group), they cultivated an arch flippancy in Cook's eyes: 'really, I'm *bored* by all that housing, I don't want to do a housing scheme, I mean it's all so dreary'.[4]

Graduating in 1971, the four came together again when Zogolovitch put together a team for **Phillips West 2**. It was the start of Campbell Zogolovitch Wilkinson and Gough, which was soon abbreviated although CZWG was hardly easier to pronounce: the architect Denys Lasdun would ask Cook 'And how are X, Y & Z?'[5] London in 1975 was a stark and bleary-eyed time to be starting out, and their ideals and enthusiasms were shocked by the

157

Piers Gough's student design for a photographer's studio, summer 1966

realities of a building site. As Gough recalled, 'You get to see exactly what happens when you build a cheap building that is trying to look expensive.'[6] Making silk purses out of sows' ears became a survival strategy for the lean years of the 1970s and early 1980s. Few architects have had their ideas put together in so many ways – from self-build to craftwork, from the stapler gun to prefabricated cladding. Finding the craft element and exploiting a special skill or material became an extension of the creative process. Stylistic development on a budget was also guided by the insight that certain architectural languages (Victorian eclecticism, for example) can be debased more convincingly than others.

Rejecting the self-referential, hermetic aspect of architectural discourse, CZWG have unashamedly drawn upon wider cultural frames of reference to devise resonant imagery. Gough introduced himself at a 1981 round-table discussion with 'I'm Piers Gough and I suppose it's true to say I desperately want to be liked'.[7] Their craving for audience recognition may stem from the public's disillusionment with architects and planners by the late 1970s. Awareness of popular as opposed to critical reception has been a stimulating rather than an inhibiting factor, yet CZWG has consistently avoided compromise or attempting to second-guess popular taste.

CZWG represented a first generation of architects for whom the patronage of the welfare state was less relevant or desirable than free enterprise. They have always enjoyed working with headstrong individuals. Early clients, such as the broadcaster Janet Street-Porter, artist Allen Jones, graphic designer Ian Logan and Tony Elliot of *Time Out* magazine, were friends and contacts from the London scene. This circle was enlarged by Roger Zogolovitch, always in search of new opportunities and clients; he was one of the first architects to become a developer after RIBA relaxed its regulations on professional practice in 1981.

Conversion of a warehouse at 33–5 Gresse Street in Fitzrovia, by CZWG, 1982–3

CZWG cut their teeth converting inner-city warehouses and factories for creative industries, following the trend for loft living established in 1970s New York and San Francisco. These early 'live/work' units helped to loosen up planning regulations on the conversion of industrial buildings for use by artists, designers, and the advertising and fashion trades. The first such conversion in London, a Smithfield hat factory, was brought by a group of artists and designers in 1979. It was followed by a warehouse conversion in Gresse Street in Fitzrovia, on which Wilkinson traced big circles across the grid of windows. Of the inherited structures Gough remarks, 'We learnt to play along with them; not to make them into something that they weren't'.[8]

Zogolovitch brought the firm into contact with a new breed of entrepreneur. For Andrew Wadsworth, then in his mid-twenties, CZWG designed the penthouse at New Concordia Wharf, **China Wharf, The Circle** and the unrealized Jacobs Island (1986). Running in parallel was a series of commissions for Keith Preston of Kentish Homes, culminating in **Cascades**. On occasion, the practice's willingness to work for commercial developers and volume house builders and adopt such techniques as fast-track construction and design and build attracted criticism from their architect peers, yet it anticipated the profession's direction of travel.

Given their desire to engage with the public on their own terms, it is ironic how few civic projects have been entrusted to the practice, notwithstanding the popularity of the **Westbourne Grove Public Conveniences**, the Green Bridge over the Mile End Road (2000), the Maggie's Centre in Nottingham (2011) and Canada Water Library (2011). It has been more successful with another form of institutional commission – exhibition design; notably with the 1981–2 Lutyens Exhibition at the Hayward Gallery, Alfred Gilbert at the Royal Academy in 1986 and the Regency, Victorian and Early Twentieth Century Galleries at the National Portrait Gallery.

CZWG's eclecticism and capacity for self-reinvention seem to defy categorization. One clue to their approach lies in James Gowan's oft-stated maxim, to use 'the style for the job': a starting point is suggested by the constraints and opportunities of the project rather than imposed by extrinsic notions. The attitude enjoyed currency in the post-war AA (where Gowan was a respected tutor) and chimed with the empirical and anti-theoretical tendencies of English architecture.

A 'style for the job' is only as good as the stylist's ability to articulate a distinctive sense of place. In Britain, contextualism came to be associated with a loss of nerve, resulting in a 'keeping in keeping' approach that tends towards homogeneity. CZWG turned the equation around, instead employing urban character as the straight man for exaggeration or juxtaposition. Contrariety is the active ingredient in **The Circle**'s glossy blue drum: its impact depends on the stock brick character of the surrounding streets. Burlesque rather than pastiche defines Gough's take on Norman Shaw at **Bryanston**; Arts and Crafts at Garden Corner on Chelsea Embankment (1978); and wharfside vernacular in the Docklands work. People and the more intangible aspects of character can provide the impulse: the 'Bling Bling building' (2006) is CZWG's love letter to Liverpool, described by Gough as 'a spectacularly and gorgeously vulgar place – the Three Graces, the swagger of the people, their language, their attitude'.[9]

That CZWG's imagery is singular is not to deny their sources: the parts are sometimes copied but the whole represents a free style entirely of their own invention. Some of their work displays a nostalgia for retro-Edwardian, debased suburbiana (sunburst gates, sub-Voysey semis) or the motor-moderne style that flourished in the 1930s along London's Great West Road; indeed, one of the alternative working titles for their 1988 monograph was *Learning from Metroland*. Their tastes in architects unsurprisingly run to those excluded from the Modern Movement canon but who found a new popularity in the 1960s; in particular Hector Guimard, Victor Horta, Michel de Klerk and Hans Poelzig. A whole sequence of projects pays homage to Guimard's entrances to the Paris Métro: the Bourne at Gerrards Cross (1983–5), **Westbourne Grove Public Conveniences** and, in abstracted form, the butterfly roof of their café at Brindleyplace, Birmingham (1997). Underlying the practice's attraction to Art Nouveau and Expressionism was the combination of freedom and novelty that resulted from transcending historicism. 'I think it's pathetic, this raiding of history, I despise it', Gough said in a 1983 interview. 'I do it because there's nothing else and I haven't invented a new vocabulary yet'.[10]

For the early conversion projects such as **Phillips West 2** and a penthouse for developer Andrew Wadsworth at New Concordia Wharf (1983–5), CZWG developed an accretive technique of layering and loading up in reaction to the emerging post-industrial aesthetic of stripped-back surfaces and sand-blasted brickwork. A tendency to elaborate rather than simplify is evident in the applied metalwork that characterizes many projects and the flying trellises of the **Janet Street-Porter House**. Interiors for *Time Out*'s offices (1978) combined neon signage and expanded metal lathes in a punk style, with partitions of sawn-up flush doors and overhead services carried down on dodgem-car contact poles. Here, cheap materials, industrial products and DIY techniques were redeemed through surreal, out-of-context juxtaposition or *bricolage* technique in the manner of Frank Gehry's early work or the 'as found' aesthetic of the New Brutalists.

Sweeping geometric figures, supergraphics and sky-signs have endured since the AA period. So, too, have exaggerations of scale: command of gesture can carry the idea along if the finishes are bland or coarse. Circular geometry is endlessly manipulated into cylinders (Bankside Lofts, 1998), quadrants (**The Circle**; Gresse Street, 1983), arcs (the Glass Building in Camden, 2000 – referencing Horta's Hôtel Tassel in Brussels), elevated circles (Lonsdale Studios, Barnsbury, 1984) and intersecting ellipses (Brindleyplace Café, Birmingham, 1997; the Nottingham Maggie's Centre, 2011).

CZWG are storytellers. The freewheeling, anecdotal quality of their architecture may have developed from the AA ritual of the 'crit' or design review, where work is presented to a jury of tutors and visiting professionals. An ever-present wit takes various forms: some designs offer observational riffs in the manner of the 1980s stand-up comedian Ben Elton; others are one-liners. Of the latter Gough is unapologetic, telling Deyan Sudjic, 'We do B-movies too, we don't just stick to features, B-movies in the sense that they have a straightforward story and not too much intellectual weight'.[11] The self-consciously anti-intellectual stance is very English, but more English still is the use of self-deprecating humour as defence, and of wit as a smoke screen for an underlying thoughtfulness.

Phillips West 2

10 Salem Road, Bayswater, City of Westminster
1975–6, CZWG

From the workaday commission of a warehouse conversion for Phillips, the London auctioneers, CZWG contrived an outré yet pragmatic statement of intent. They described their design in terms of post-modernist 'loading up' rather than the 'stripping back' of the Modern Movement.[12] The ground floor of the T-plan building was taken up with an open-plan auction room. By adding a set-back storey to the frontage building, seven maisonettes (a planning condition) were squeezed in. Their front doors are reached from a first-floor courtyard, with lettable offices to the rear.

This improvisational, ad-hoc design evokes the former bohemianism of Bayswater Road and the freedom opened up by the 1970s' package holiday boom. The street front freely evoked a Costa Brava mood, with ice-cream pink walls, exotic ironwork and a broad-brimmed, pantile roof. Gough explained how 'the planners thought it was Frank Lloyd Wright we had in mind; therefore they insisted that it should be painted brown or maroon. … So we did it pink'.[13] The scrolling balcony ironwork echoes a similar detail at the neighbouring Edwardian mansion house, while the entrance canopy, now sadly removed, featured Guimard's whiplash forms. The colonnaded rear patio was more Roman in feel, while the maisonettes were given swooping brick walls and stair handrails.

Phillips West 2 has since been repainted a bland off-white, and its ground-floor openings altered.

Janet Street-Porter House

Britton Street, Clerkenwell, Islington, London
1986–8, CZWG

Piers Gough, Janet Street-Porter and Mike Di Marco – architect, client,
builder – met at the Architectural Association in 1965, although Street-Porter
soon dropped out and moved on to journalism and youth TV. The products of
a counter-cultural era, the three co-created a celebration of 'left-over sixties
optimism'.[14] Of Gough's initial sketches, Street-Porter chose the one that she
thought elegant, spiky and tough. The result is a restless, strident portrait of
the exchange between architect and client.

    The default residential format of stock brick, pitched roof and regular
hole-in-wall windows is playfully subverted. Effect is piled upon effect: the
trompe-l'oeil brickwork (Street-Porter's idea), the art-nouveau-ish metalwork
balconies, and the diagonal grid slicing through the building to leave
diamond panes, sloping sills and jutting trellis work (an oblique homage to
Frank Gehry's house in Santa Monica). The concrete tree-trunk lintels allude
to Marc-Antoine Laugier's concept of primitive architecture and the London
Building Acts, while the films of Orson Welles inspired the dark timber doors
with their rope handles and ham-Gothic ironmongery.

    Instead of a front door a gateway gives onto a small entrance courtyard.
The tension between the diagonal geometry of the canted street corner and
the curved back wall (the result of a need to preserve 'ancient lights') is a
unifying theme, where each storey has a different layout. At the top, the
penthouse office is reached via an external staircase that was requested
to help separate work from play. Street-Porter's interiors were equally
idiosyncratic and brash, combining raw concrete and dyed plaster finishes.
Unsurprisingly, they failed to outlast their original occupant when she moved
into a Clerkenwell house designed by David Adjaye.

Craft Design and Technology Building

Bryanston School, Blandford Forum, Dorset
1986–8, CZWG

Bryanston School occupies a colossal house of 1889–94 by R Norman Shaw as well as extensive buildings erected in the grounds since the 1950s. At interview for the commission of a detached crafts building, Gough presented no drawings but proposed an entirely different site, instigating a new eastern courtyard on axis with Shaw's east wing that was less disruptive to the old house and its setting. He won the job.

The first-floor layout of double-pile classrooms open to a barrel roof is expressed in the gable ends, whose scale and quoin detailing are bold enough to stand up to Shaw. A semi-circular recess (designed for a tree which failed to survive the construction process) marks the main entrance. The entrance front is punctuated with a giant order in cast stone resembling the screw columns of a G-clamp. These support hooded windows (an allusion to the computers then being introduced to design courses) and mortar boards. Ever the pragmatists, CZWG reused the column moulds for their own Clerkenwell offices, where they are painted gold.

CZWG were invited back to Bryanston in 1995 to design a pair of boarding houses in a single butterfly-plan block. A more significant mark of the success of their CDT block (now renamed the Gough Building) is that Hopkins Architects' later Sanger Centre is planned in relation to it and its eastern courtyard.

China Wharf

29 Mill Street, Tower Bridge, Southwark, London
Designed 1982–3, built 1986–8, CZWG

In 1980, the 23-year-old Andrew Wadsworth bought New Concordia Wharf, a derelict Bermondsey warehouse, and carried out the first residential conversion in Docklands. He commissioned CZWG to convert its former water tower into his penthouse apartment, then asked them to design a residential building on the adjoining site. This became China Wharf, a name evoking the unloading of exotic cargoes – it actually commemorates Wadsworth's cat, China. Gough planned 17 flats on a complex 'scissor-section', with interlocking dwellings stepping over a central corridor. This gave each flat riverside views from the living rooms and bedrooms on the landward side. The scheme was approved by Ted Hollamby, the architect-planner for the London Docklands Development Corporation, despite his apprehensions of an 'Odeon on the Thames'.

Each elevation is quite distinct, reflecting the different aspects of this tight infill site. Cantilevered out over the river is a stack of Baroque scallops, a concrete/metal composite structure from which projects nautical balconies. The exuberant top arch echoes Otto Wagner's *Jugendstil* Karlsplatz Stadtbahn Station in Vienna. The poppy red façade is a focal point on the riverscape, like the Thames sailing barges that were once an everyday presence here. At the rear, white-painted flutes, like an inside-out grain silo or an unrolled ionic column, accommodate angled windows in order to avoid overlooking. The intervening gable wall draws directly on the wharfside vernacular; the neighbouring Reeds Wharf seems to emerge from its loophole frame. The result is one of the few 20th-century buildings to fully realize the architectural possibilities of the Thames. Combining exuberant geometry and Docklands contextualism, China Wharf represents the high tide of British post-modernism.

The Circle

Queen Elizabeth Street, Shad Thames, Southwark, London
1987–9, CZWG

A theatrical gesture at the heart of a speculative development, The Circle
is an urbane piece of post-modern placemaking. Andrew Wadsworth (the
developer of **China Wharf**) bought the site from Whitbread's brewery; the
connection is commemorated by Shirley Pace's bronze sculpture *Jacob – The
Circle Dray Horse*. Wadsworth asked for two separate designs on each side of
Queen Elizabeth Street so he could sell one off, but Gough could not resist
designing a single entity. He conceived a focal point like a circus, compressed
down to a dense, powerful space. Significantly, The Circle predated the blue
ceramic drum of Stirling Wilford's **1 Poultry**.

Gough imagined the narrow streets of Shad Thames as man-made
canyons, carved from a solid stratum of stock brick. If you discovered this
precious seam of lapis lazuli, he reasoned, you would quarry it out, so
enlarging the space. The volume enclosed is about the same as a gasholder,
but Gough was also thinking of ceramic storage vessels; hence the neck or
rim at the top. The builders immediately dubbed them 'the owls'– a name
that stuck, to Gough's bemusement. Away from the glazed brick edge, the
development settles into a rhythmic Docklands streetscape, enlivened by zig-
zagging balconies and a wavy parapet.

The construction period succeeded Black Monday (19 October 1987) but
the ensuing recession mattered little; all but ten of the 314 units had been
sold before work began. 'People want to live in a special place,' Gough says;
'they want people to say "oh you live *there*!"'

Cascades

4 Westferry Road, Isle of Dogs, Tower Hamlets, London
1987–8, CZWG

Cascades is the culmination of a dozen London schemes that CZWG designed for Keith Preston of builder–developers Kentish Homes. Its site in Sufferance Wharf was purchased in 1985 with planning permission for three- and four-storey houses. Visiting Hong Kong, Rex Wilkinson had been impressed by the potent compound of property speculation and a waterside situation. It was not hard to persuade the 'frustrated architect' Preston and the London Docklands Development Corporation that what the site needed was a tall building.[15] The first Canary Wharf skyscrapers provided a planning precedent for breaking through the local authority's height limit but with its fast-track construction, Cascades bears the palm as Dockland's first high-rise development.

The irony that the 20-storey building, dubbed 'yuppie towers', was rising from the ground at the same time that Ronan Point was being dynamited was not lost on CZWG. Every part of Cascades – its ramped profile, concertina plan and brick cladding – is worked hard to sell high-rise living to middle-class consumers. Preston wanted the development to have the feel of an international hotel, with a concierge, shops and residents' facilities. A series of penthouses is clustered along the sloping edge, its south-facing orientation permitting a cascade of sun terraces and London's most dramatic fire escape route. The highest point of the building hails Canary Wharf, grading down to lower neighbours to the south. A fragmented mix of imagery – a Docklands coal conveyor, ocean liners, warehouse remnants at the base – is sprinkled across the heroic form. CZWG reprised the concertina plan and ski-jump silhouette for their Steedman Street apartments at London's Elephant and Castle in 2005.

200–260
Aztec West

Almondsbury, Bristol
1987–8, CZWG

Aztec West was one of the first out of town business parks, drawing tenants from nearby Bristol and the high-technology M4 corridor. Like John Outram's nearby **1200 Park Avenue**, CZWG's design pointedly departs from the tinny sheds that populated Bruce Gilbreth Architects' master plan. To celebrate the motor car as the begetter of this building type and lend an air of drama to arrival and departure, Piers Gough based the circular entrance courts on a car's turning circle. Resembling twin square doughnuts with nibbled corners, the plan could be realized in two stages and was shallow enough to be subdivided into small office suites.

Souped up with bands of red and buff brick – the architectural equivalent of go-faster stripes – Rex Wilkinson's façades invoke the speed and vulgarity of 'Jazz modern'. The giant order of columns (in the manner of Ricardo Bofill's Noisy-le-Grand housing in Paris) is counterbalanced by a high parapet with pre-cast trimmings. When the sweeping curve of the drum hits a straight edge the resulting 'flat-iron' effect is reminiscent of a film set. And the entrance – extruded Art Deco lettering projecting over a half moon – is pure Hollywood.

Westbourne Grove Public Conveniences

Royal Borough of Kensington and Chelsea, London
1993, CZWG

Until the Maggie's Centre at Nottingham and the Canada Water Library, both completed in 2011, these elegant loos were CZWG's only public work and were the initiative of local residents. The firm was approached by John Scott after his Pembridge Association took exception to the downbeat classical conveniences proposed by Kensington and Chelsea council. Gough's design was accepted after Scott made up the £20,000 difference between the estimates. Gough credits the recession for the fact that such a lavish structure could be realized within a comparatively meagre budget, while the group raised extra funds to donate a bespoke aluminium clock, lamp post and bench.

CZWG designed a new triangular traffic island, landscaped with trees, benches and Yorkstone paving. On this sits a pavilion of similar shape, clad with the turquoise glazed bricks more normally used to clad the interiors of public toilets. A translucent canopy is jauntily cantilevered from the steel frame. Its parallel sides swell out as the building narrows, creating a forced perspective effect and sweeping around the corner. The dancing figures identifying the 'ladies'' and 'gents'' are inspired by the Notting Hill carnival, which passes by annually. It was Scott's idea to incorporate a glazed florist's kiosk, the rental income from which offsets the cost of a lavatory attendant.

John Outram

John Outram's architecture has a classical bravura, with many elements over-scaled and brilliantly coloured. It may appear outlandish, but it is informed by both a complex iconography and the astute understanding of budgets, materials and services that make his buildings supremely practical.

Outram (1934–) was born in Malaysia, the only child of an English aide-de-camp. Arriving in England in 1946, he attended Wellington College, traditionally a preparation for a military career. However, two years of national service with the Royal Air Force in Canada impelled him instead towards architecture. He worked for a summer in the hotel bar at Portmeirion, North Wales, where he encountered Clough Williams-Ellis and Frank Lloyd Wright and then, with £50 from his father and a £300 scholarship, entered Regent Street Polytechnic in 1955, an exciting time to be studying architecture.

At the school he met his wife Rima Finiefs, a fellow student. With their contemporaries, they visited Le Corbusier's newly completed chapel at Ronchamp, which influenced Outram's free-form, sometimes machine-inspired architecture. Its curved or stepped façades were determined by what lay within, and the style has been accordingly termed Bowellism. Outram with Wilfred Marden launched a student magazine, *Polygon*, in 1956, worried at the lack of theory in their architectural training.[1] They published the best-known Bowellist scheme, by Michael Webb, two years ahead at the school and later one of the founders of Archigram. Their tutor, Bill Howell, encouraged the pair to apply for scholarships to the more prestigious Architectural Association (AA), where the fifth-year master Peter Smithson introduced them to Louis Kahn and suggested other directions than those of Le Corbusier, Mies and Frank Lloyd Wright. Outram's thesis tutor was Bob Maxwell, who persuaded the AA to pass his third attempt (a version of

John Outram outside the New House at Wadhurst Park, c.1985, photographed by his father

Churchill College) after more ambitious schemes for rebuilding Croydon and for a motorway-based community had been rejected.

Outram joined the London County Council and worked for four years on its programme for expanding Huntingdon, but was dispirited by its inefficiency and lack of ideas. He assisted Fitzroy Robinson on the London Stock Exchange and Louis de Soissons in rebuilding the terraces round Regents Park, where he learned about traditional construction while absorbing himself in a growing collection of antiquarian books. Outram was bewitched by the major exhibition on Claude Lorrain he saw in 1968, finding architectural possibilities in his iconic narrative. Many of Claude's paintings feature river landscapes, perhaps symbolizing the 'river of life', a symbolism that Outram's architecture also expresses (notably his **Isle of Dogs Pumping Station**). Outram also extended Claude's use of classical sources to more ancient mythologies, particularly Vedic cosmogony, perhaps the earliest creation myth, and evolved a series of abstract geometric icons that informed the decoration of his later buildings.

Outram set up his own practice, but a plan to move to Cyprus was thwarted by the Turkish invasion of 1974, leaving him with only a little interior design work for Rima's family in London. Fortunes changed with a warehouse at Poyle near Heathrow for **McKay Securities**. Outram found that a steel or concrete frame clad in brick and timber, roofed with sheet metal or (preferably) clay tiles, with details cast in concrete or terrazzo, could be adapted to any solution and made attractive. His first job introduced him to the contractor David Knowles, who provided the technical virtuosity to realize Outram's ideas for cast concrete, often working with Diespeker of Islington, who had been specialists in marble and terrazzo before turning to concrete. Poyle's success led to a more ambitious commission from McKay: a line of warehouses in Kensal Road, Kensington. For this project, pedimented roofs bestrode fat round columns containing most of the services, while chunky cast concrete capitals incorporated ventilation and rainwater extracts. Peter Smithson had introduced Outram to Louis Kahn's notion of using hollow columns as service ducts, and so he put all the mechanical services into a giant external 'robot order'.

Having worried that iconography and theory is rarely addressed in architecture, Outram found an effective way of expressing his thoughts on both, writing up the projects as a series of drawings resembling a cartoon strip. The *Architectural Review* and *AA Files* liked the approach and brought him to critical attention. His pedimented shed can be seen as a classical temple or a primitive raft, which he envisaged rising from primeval forests out of a dark swamp. Green for trees and particularly blue, representing water, eyes or skies, became important to his architecture, with red representing fire. The elemental symbolism of his buildings is fused with a robust classicism.

A more luxurious side to Outram's work appeared with **New House** at Wadhurst Park, commissioned in 1978, although inlaid marble floors were combined with cheap concrete techniques. The decorative concrete cladding incorporated crushed brick, based on a wartime recipe for recycling rubble that Outram had seen while working on the Regent's Park terraces. He called the process 'Blitzcrete'. For his remodelling of Wadhurst's Victorian conservatory in 1984–5 he and Knowles perfected a blue concrete using cobalt, which featured prominently in his subsequent work. Later, he developed a technique of inlaying patterns of contrasting coloured concrete slip into surface troughs created by rubber moulds, termed 'doodlecrete'. Both processes can be seen in the Millennium Pavilion at Wadhurst, added in 1999. Each column includes an octagon of green concrete, made using chromic oxide and green granite aggregate and a cluster of reeds coloured in blue and white spirals. Each is topped by an eye of lead crystal and a shiny black capital that support a steel superstructure, with copper mouldings, a blind and aluminium louvres.

The use of columns and pediments had evolved with buildings for **Harp Heating** in Swanley and the **Isle of Dogs Pumping Station**. Outram placed services in external columns, his robot order, and topped them with flame-coloured capitals. The pumping station caught the popular imagination, even if few recognized its iconography: Outram much admired Paul Ricoeur's *The Rule of Metaphor*, which in 1975 set out the idea of a river having a birth, life and death, and his three-volume *Time and Narrative* (1984–8), which explores the paradoxes of philosophy.

Outram never secured another public commission, although limited competitions for large office buildings enabled him to expand his office. The schemes were published, but nothing was built. In 1986 he was one of five

Offices, 200 Queen Victoria Street, Blackfriars, for Stuart Lipton, 1988 (not built)

architects invited to rebuild Bracken House in London and produced a design for a seven-storey office block with a stepped atrium featuring a waterfall. Externally a giant order carried the air conditioning. He also published a scheme for Paternoster Square as a series of towers growing out of the forest of the city. Similarly large offices followed at Blackfriars for Stuart Lipton of Rosehaugh Stanhope Developments, who had admired the Isle of Dogs Pumping Station. The scheme collapsed in the recession of 1990, as did a commission for headquarters for the Association of Consumer Research, publishers of *Which?* magazine. Outram was runner up for an opera house at Compton Verney and a grandstand at Epsom. In 1997 he was one of six practices appointed to design a hotel inside Battersea Power Station, and

Anne and Charles Duncan Hall (Computational Engineering Building), Rice University, Houston, Texas, 1993–7

proposed a scheme for the whole interior with shops and a cinema around a giant atrium. He also planned streets and squares for the surrounding land. However, his refusal to work with an unqualified executive designer, and the manner in which large developers sought to realize his schemes using their own fast-track building teams led him to withdraw into one-off projects.

The scale and iconography of the office schemes informed Outram's one major building in Britain, the **Judge Business School** (former Judge Institute of Management Studies) at Cambridge University, of 1991–5. It was Outram's first completed atrium, defined by his robot order. It should have been still more colourful, with a marble floor and painted ceiling, the latter developed from printing techniques devised when Outram designed an exhibition on A W N Pugin for the Victoria and Albert Museum in 1994, but the institute rejected his proposals. To see a complete Outram interior one must visit

184

Duncan Hall, the Computational Engineering Building at Rice University, Houston, Texas. He was invited to compete for the job in 1993 after the head of the building committee, Josephine Abercrombie, saw an article on the Wadhurst conservatory. Completed in 1997, the central hall linking tutorial and lecture rooms is treated as a river, with Outram producing a ceiling mural, *The Birth of Consciousness*, printed on to vinyl and described by him as a 'talking order', the best expression of his geometric icons. Its bright colours are very different to the understated classicism of James Stirling's extension to the M D Anderson Hall also at Rice.

Outram's last work was in the Netherlands, where in 2002 he converted The Hague's partly medieval Oude Stadhuis into offices for the developer MAB with a two-storey shopping centre on the site of a 1970s council chamber. Outram had earlier designed a bandstand in Maastricht, and eventually in 2010 realized a brick block of 100 apartments at Haverleij, a new town on the polders planned as a series of high-density units.

Outram stands resolutely apart from any movement, although his modernist training and rejection of traditional classicism fit him for inclusion in the post-modern canon. In 1981 he remarked that 'what Modernism needs is an equivalent to the oneiric language of Classical Architecture and Urbanism which addresses not a reality of myth populated by gods but a myth of reality populated by humans'.[2] Yet he remains entirely separate from such a movement as exists, for his work is unrelated to that of Venturi, Scott Brown, Rossi or their counterparts in other countries, but has evolved of itself since Outram completed his training in 1961. His architecture is immediately recognizable for its bright colours and three-dimensional quality, realized in traditional materials externally, all linking contemporary needs with the ancient past. For a brief moment in the late 1980s the 'otherness' of buildings like the pumping station was celebrated, but Outram quickly reverted to the role of outsider, admired by the public but little recognized by the architectural profession.

McKay Securities

Blackthorne Road, Poyle, Surrey
1974–6, John Outram Associates

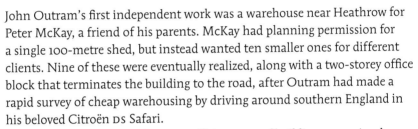

John Outram's first independent work was a warehouse near Heathrow for Peter McKay, a friend of his parents. McKay had planning permission for a single 100-metre shed, but instead wanted ten smaller ones for different clients. Nine of these were eventually realized, along with a two-storey office block that terminates the building to the road, after Outram had made a rapid survey of cheap warehousing by driving around southern England in his beloved Citroën DS Safari.

Outram found that the most efficient way of building was a simple steel frame, which he clad in soft, porous yellow brick that he contrasted with hard blue engineering brick. Each unit is a pair of arches – one forward and one back, to create a loading bay – inspired by Le Corbusier's Roc et Rob housing project of 1948 and Louis Kahn's Kimbell Art Gallery, completed in 1972. The façades, including the timber windows, are entirely flat. They feature Outram's first concrete capital, cast by David Knowles, with whom he worked on all his subsequent buildings. This incorporates a number, a floodlight to illuminate the loading bay and a gutter overflow – the latter two make up an exclamation mark and are a modest prototype for Outram's later robot order. His concern for detail extended to the choice of interlocking brick setts as neater than asphalt for the forecourt and loading bays.

The project's success led to a second, more elaborate group of warehouses for McKay in Kensal Road, Kensington, demolished c.2004.

New House

Wadhurst Park, near Tunbridge Wells, East Sussex
Designed 1978–81, built 1982–6; conservatory roof 1988, 2007;
Millennium Pavilion 1999; John Outram Associates

Hans Rausing, retired owner of the packaging company Tetra Pak, bought
Wadhurst Park to avoid Swedish tax, and to breed deer. He had promised
his wife Märit a house, and was introduced to John Outram through a
local landscape architect, Anthony du Gard Pasley. They wanted something
'sophisticated but not wacky', explains Outram, who showed them his one
completed building, at Poyle. The ultimate source for the project was Louis
Kahn's Kimbell Art Gallery.

Outram designed a single-storey house on a raised terrace, its high
ceilings related to the conservatory that survived from a Victorian house
previously on the site, and also to accommodate Rausing's 6ft 7in height.
The H-plan was arranged around a dark entrance hall, its inlaid floor
representing the dials of a giant compass, with a saloon to the rear, bedrooms
and a library on one side, and the dining room and kitchen on the other
adjoining the conservatory, which was first roofed over for the wedding of the
Rausings' eldest daughter.

The exterior is most striking. The steel frame is clad in bands of brick
and travertine, divided into the bays of the underlying grid by piers of
blitzcrete concrete with lacquered black capitals, robotic volutes containing
lights and overflows, and tall chimneys. A pattern of bricks, concrete and
travertine on the terrace delineates the building's 90cm grid, and also defines
the Millennium Pavilion. This colourful veranda, added in 1999, encapsulates
all Outram's iconography and forms a contrast to his earlier 'living order' of
plants in open piers.

Harp Heating

United House, Swanley, Kent
1982–4, John Outram Associates, demolished 2016

When working for Louis de Soissons in the early 1970s, Outram met the heating engineer Geoffrey Granter, a specialist in installing central heating in council housing. He needed offices and warehousing for his flat-pack kits, and found some cheap but run-down 1960s premises at Swanley that were convenient for the M25 motorway. Outram strengthened the floors and extended the concrete frame of the frontage 'gatehouse' building in steel. He then wrapped both buildings in brick and tiles, with wooden windows sheltered from the sun by deep eaves and projecting blinds, and added pitched tiled roofs.

Most importantly, Outram added columns to the long elevations. These were set in threes, of which the central one had no structural pier at its rear. They housed the services, including a shower for the managing director, and thus ensured that they did not interfere with the lettable volume. The columns featured capitals with flame motifs – appreciated as a joke by Harp's service engineers if not by the architectural cognoscenti. Outram then treated the end gables as pediments, into which he inserted a thermostatically controlled loft-ventilating fan that he described as the solar cave of somatic time. The staircases featured cast terrazzo, with a timber handrail inspired by Le Corbusier resting on angled chrome balusters that were indebted to Louis Kahn.

1200 Park Avenue

Aztec West Business Park, Patchway, Gloucestershire
1984–6, John Outram Associates

Aztec West was an unusually ambitious industrial estate near the junction of the M4 and M5 motorways, planned following American models. The client was Richard Ellis, acting on behalf of the Electricity Supply Nominees' pension fund, who in 1980 commissioned a master plan from Farrell, Grimshaw & Partners. However, high-tech rapidly gave way to cheap design-and-build modules that proved easy to let. Outram's work restored Ellis's ambition, showing that brick skin construction on a light steel frame with pitched roofs of fibre cement sheeting could be cheaper than prefabricated structures, yet remain durable and attractive, especially when ennobled with engaged columns and broken pediments. The scheme repeats many of the features found in the warehousing at Kensington.

Outram's block comprises 3,500m² of warehousing on a triangular plan, stepped on one side to follow the curve of Park Avenue. There are 12 units ranging in size from 53 to 131m², and they were completed in 37 weeks. There are three broken pediments to front and back, originally with eye-like lights, each half-pediment serving a warehouse with a tall garage door and a two-storey office area. The double-height glazed windows and door were originally painted red, but have since been renewed in grey. The engaged columns of contrasting brick incorporate services, now the earliest examples of Outram's robot order. Cast concrete capitals between the pediments incorporate waterspouts and there are more castings for the warehouse numbers, produced by Stone of Stroud, manufacturers of bird baths.

Isle of Dogs Pumping Station

Stewart Street, Tower Hamlets
1986–8, John Outram Associates; listed Grade II* in 2017

Edward Hollamby, architect to the Docklands Development Corporation, liked the Kensington warehouses and so gave Outram one of only two public commissions that were in his gift. The brief was for a building that could last 100 years without on-site supervision, being required simply to cover the concrete chambers where floodwater and sewage are pumped up and discharged into the River Thames. The engineers, William Halcrow and Partners, determined the plan of an aisled hall. This lurks tantalisingly behind massive battered brick walls that conceal a grey brick transformer station, also by Outram.

Outram's steel frame is clad in bands of Staffordshire blue engineering bricks, Redland Otterham stocks and Butterley Rochford red facing bricks. A concrete dado supports cast columns and eaves brackets, while at the gable ends giant semi-circular columns conceal ventilation ducts. Pre-cast concrete fins form Corinthian capitals two metres high, coloured by black aggregate or painted in primary colours. Electrically operated fans in the pediments at either end prevent the build-up of methane gas, while appearing as a Cyclopean eye. Each pediment can also be interpreted as the source of a river, depicted as ripples by the lines of contrasting coloured brickwork down the elevations. Moreover, the complete structure can be understood as a funeral pyre floating on the River Nile, for Outram embodying both the origins of the earth and the course of life from birth to death.

195

Judge Business School

Trumpington Street, Cambridge
Designed 1991–2, built 1993–5, John Outram Associates

When Sir Paul Judge and the Honourable Simon Sainsbury founded a business school in the 19th-century Old Addenbrooke's Hospital building in Cambridge they determined to commission an ambitious and eye-catching architecture that would stand out amongst the refined post-war modernism of much of the university's 20th-century building.

Outram was invited to enter a limited competition by Colin Amery. His winning scheme converted the listed hospital ward blocks into a library and seminar rooms. He enclosed the linking arcades and incorporated a 1907 rooftop extension that had been proposed for demolition, gaining valuable space and unifying the overall composition with a cornice, blue columns and red dentils. To the rear, Outram added new buildings: the Ark, containing offices for tutors, research graduates and administrative staff, and the Castle, housing the main auditorium and debating room rising out of a dark base or 'heap of history' with working columns he described as pillars of fire. The Gallery, a newly built internal atrium containing a café and seminar spaces with staircases that lead to a roof garden over the Ark, links old and new elements. Services and lighting were installed inside giant columns. The height of the main spaces and the setting back of the glazing preclude the need for air conditioning, while the thick walls and ceilings maintain an even temperature.

The donors rejected Outram's scheme for a ceiling mural that would have completed his iconography, to be replaced instead by a tessellation of closed irises. A scheme of planting and turf for the roof garden was also cut; nevertheless the building exudes an architectural lushness.

Sphinx Hill

Moulsford, Oxfordshire
Designed 1994 onwards, built 1998–9, John Outram Associates

Outram designed one other house after **New House** at Wadhurst Park, for Christopher and Henrietta McCall. They approached him after seeing his Isle of Dogs pumping station – Henrietta McCall is an Egyptologist – but it was only in 1997 that they found the perfect riverside site, replacing a 1970s house.

Sphinx Hill is constructed of blockwork, with symmetrical façades and three arched copper roofs, the central one higher. The house is broad rather than tall, and partly only single storey. For the upper parts, David Knowles's blue cobalt concrete responds to the sky, while a new coloured render with black and white flecks and a scraped finish enlivens the texture. Flat capitals formed of red circles over black petals symbolize the sun as well as denoting the beam ends of the roof.

The centrepiece of the ground floor is a cross-vaulted dining room with pilasters and a floor of Egyptian limestone. To the side is a swimming pool – blue with gold capitals – a mosaic floor and a segmental vault of stretched Mylar polyester sheeting, chosen to avoid condensation. The first-floor drawing room has a pyramid fire and pilasters containing uplighters that repeat the simple stylized capitals. It is a small house, but consistent in its iconography.

The formal gardens feature a narrow canal called the Nile, lined with paired sphinxes. Yet the Thameside setting remains quintessentially English, which only enhances the building's novelty. Outram told *Country Life* magazine that 'We are the only architect's practice who believes that tradition and modernity can be joined to make a singular novelty'.[3]

East Workshops

The Harley Studios, Welbeck Estate, near Worksop,
Nottinghamshire
2000, John Outram Associates

Ivy Cavendish-Bentinck, Duchess of Portland, began to develop Welbeck
Abbey's 22 acres of kitchen gardens with craft workshops in 1977; a
garden centre and café were later added. An area on the west side of the
walled garden had been laid out in the 19th century with hot water pipes
and manure pits for cultivating pineapples; it was here, in 2000, that
Outram built nine lean-to workshops for £750/m², after Arts Lottery funding
had been withdrawn. Tucked between a long drive and the kitchen wall, the
U-shaped terrace (sometimes known as Pineapple Place) houses
an isolated but close community. It forms a street of joy in the eerie landscape
of Welbeck Abbey, where beyond the walled gardens and Victorian gas works
lurk miles of semi-submerged tunnels created for the reclusive fifth
Duke of Portland.

Outram's buildings were constructed cheaply of concrete block, timber
and render behind a steel frame, each with a large entrance for moving
equipment or artworks as well as a formal door for visitors. The roofs angle
sharply downwards, making them invisible from within the Victorian kitchen
garden as was required by the planners. The interiors are simple and flexible,
interrupted only by red-painted steel columns and timber mezzanines. But
the fronts are high, bold and strong. They have Outram's clearest palette of
colours and the most intelligible of his mature iconographies, in which the
brown and green columns represent the primeval forest appearing from the
water, the yellow squares suns or primitive beam ends, and the red timber
entablature a flaming raft.

Legacy

Page 206: 'A House for Essex', Wrabness, north Essex, by Fashion Architecture Taste in collaboration with Grayson Perry, 2014–15

The sudden eclipse of post-modernism in the 1990s left unanswered questions about its lasting contribution to British architecture. As a style, its passing was regretted by few, yet its extensive critical and theoretical armoury continues to be exploited in different ways. Perhaps post-modernism left a permissive space in British architecture. While genres such as deconstructivism, high-tech, and minimalism continue to represent points of convergence, British architecture culture has arguably become less tribal and increasingly pluralistic. Unaffiliated to any single ideology, architects can today dip in and out of different formal languages to respond to the contingencies of context and programme. It is a situation that can be traced back to the architecture of Alison and Peter Smithson, who devised radically different languages while working on the Sugden House in Watford and House of the Future simultaneously in 1955–6.

What, then, is the legacy of post-modernism? Perhaps it is less about the revival of forms than the continuing relevance of underlying tactics and propositions. Charles Jencks has argued that after a period of 1990s exile the post-modern movement has returned in all but name, citing phenomena such as digital ornament, the iconic building and the urban layering of the 'time city'.[1] In 'Radical Post-modernism', a special issue of *Architectural Design*, Jencks, together with Sean Griffiths, Charles Holland and Sam Jacob of Fashion Architecture Taste (FAT), characterize post-modernism as 'an incomplete project'.[2] They identify a toolbox of post-modernist concerns and tactics, including figuration, ornament, narrative and iconography, which offer a means of communication with users and the public. Their post-modernism is a continuation of the modernist project by other means: its techniques of collage, juxtaposition, layering and quotation were prevalent in modernist art and literature but failed to transfer across to the International Style of architecture in the 1930s.

School of Slavonic and East European Studies, University College London,
by Short and Associates, 2003–5

Architectural legacies stem from networks of influence and inheritance.
Many notable architects emerged from the Stirling Wilford office. The 1989
open competition for **Avenue de Chartres Car Park** was Andrew Birds,
Richard Portchmouth and Mike Russum's opportunity to establish their
own practice. Stirling's influence is manifest in its contextual references,
calculated ambiguity of scale and brightly coloured accents. The influence of
Aldo Rossi and Léon Krier (a former Stirling protégé) was more detectable in
the subsequent work of the Dublin architects John Tuomey, Sheila O'Donnell
and Paul Keogh, including Tuomey's Abbotstown laboratory (1985) and

children's court in Smithfield, Dublin (1987) and Keogh's project for regional administrative offices at Tralee. The trio organized a 1983 exhibition of Aldo Rossi's work at the Blue Studio in Dublin.

A baroque sensuality and a sense of unfolding movement characterizes the eclectic output of Nigel Coates, which combines architecture with the design of interiors, exhibitions and furniture. Studying at the AA in 1972–4, Coates was influenced by performance art and the radical Italian collectives Archizoom and Superstudio. From 1980 he led the school's Diploma Unit 10, and from their radical, post-punk reimagining of London street culture in 1983 emerged the NATØ (Narrative Architecture Today) collective. In partnership with Doug Branson from 1985 to 2006, Coates worked on several Japanese projects, including Caffè Bongo, Tokyo (1986) and Noah's Ark restaurant, Sapporo (1988). His built work in Britain includes the **Geffrye Museum extension**, the Oyster House (both 1998) and the National Centre for Popular Music in Sheffield (1999), now the Hubs music venue of Sheffield Hallam University.

The work of Alan Short stands apart for different reasons. A partner at Edward Cullinan Architects from 1980–6 and subsequently in partnership with Tony Peake (1986–92) and Brian Ford (1992–6), Short's practice is closely intertwined with his academic research. His study of low-energy design strategies has generated a sequence of extrovert forms that include the **Queen's Building** at De Montfort University, Leicester (1991–3); the Contact Theatre, Manchester (1997–9); Lanchester Library, Coventry University (1998–2000) and the School of Slavonic and East European Studies, University College London (2003–5). Short's decorated brick manner relates to the Amsterdam School and the work of the Philadelphia architect Frank Furness, while his cowled ventilation stacks recall Gaudí's thrusting chimneys and towers.

The potential of post-modernism for subversion and irony – never fully explored in 1980s Britain – was belatedly fulfilled by Fashion Architecture Taste (FAT), a collaborative that was active from the early 1990s to 2014. Sharing Robert Venturi and Denise Scott Brown's interest in the ugly and the ordinary, FAT collide high cultural references with mass culture, filtered through a pop art sensibility. They sought to appropriate and reclaim a style that had become so consumed and commodified that it was by the early 1990s unmentionable amongst architects. Like conceptual artists they simultaneously occupied a provocative aesthetic position while providing a deadpan commentary on it. Their 1995 chill-out room for the Brunel Rooms nightclub in Swindon, in which clubbers relaxed amongst chintz armchairs and plush curtains like those in their parents' living rooms, was an early exploration of popular taste cultures that later, at **Islington Square**, was put to use in the design of social housing. Griffiths's **Blue House** and the 2008

villa at Hoogvliet, one of several projects in the Netherlands, both apply mannerist formal techniques of exaggeration and distortions of scale and proportion to billboard-like façades.

Like many British post-modernists, FAT were at their boldest when responding to historic contexts, such as their office for the advertising agency Kesselskramer which colonizes a 19th-century Amsterdam church (1998) or *You Make Me Feel Mighty Real* (2000), a Romanesque folly of shimmering blue sequins designed for an exhibition at Belsay Hall, Northumberland in 2000 and now installed in the Grisedale Forest. With Crimson Architectural Historians, they remixed the material culture of post-war Britain for *A Clockwork Jerusalem*, the British contribution to the 2014 Venice Architecture Biennale. *A House for Essex* (2014–15), designed in collaboration with the artist Grayson Perry, was FAT's parting shot yet suggested new points of departure, including English domestic architecture and the narrative potential of the Arts and Crafts tradition. The building's omission from the 2016 RIBA Stirling prize shortlist was a reconfirmation of FAT's outsider status.

A flowering of contextual pattern and ornament at the turn of the century suggests the absorption of post-modern tropes into the modernist mainstream of British architecture. Decoration can today be outsourced through collaborations with artists (in much the same way as post-war architects commissioned murals or sculpture for their buildings) and its production is facilitated by digital modelling and fabrication technologies. Caruso St John's 2002–7 entrance pavilion to the V&A Bethnal Green Museum of Childhood features geometric inlays of red quartzite, brown porphyries and creamy Ancaster limestone, designed with the artist Simon Moretti. In the same practice's Nottingham Contemporary (2004–9), green, lace-etched concrete cladding references the city's Lace Market.

In the hands of some designers, a deliberately 'façadist' approach offers a critique of the constraints of modern construction techniques and procurement practices. The procurement of athletes' housing for the 2012 London Olympics was rationalized, with one team devising a standardized plan, structure and services and others appointed to design cladding for the ten-storey courtyard blocks. A façade by Níall McLaughlin Architects reproduces fragments of galloping horses from the Parthenon Frieze, which were laser scanned and converted into modular pre-cast relief panels.

A commitment to the public realm is a defining concern for socially committed architects. Interdisciplinary practices such as muf architecture/ art, DK-CM, Assemble and Public Works collaborate with cultural institutions, regeneration agencies and community groups, funded by urban renewal initiatives, which were a priority of the Labour Governments of 1997–2010. The outcomes might be either temporary or permanent, occupying the territory between installation, community activism and master planning. In the regeneration process, local histories and landmarks are reworked to create new meanings, unify different agendas and repair degraded places. The 2005–8 landscaping of Barking Town Square by muf architecture/art included a folly wall, as an ironic commentary on the role of heritage in urban renewal. Constructed from reclaimed bricks by apprentices from Barking College, it incorporates Victorian architectural fragments and animal sculpture.

Additions to historic buildings and sites have long encouraged a more licentious and thought-provoking approach than might be justified elsewhere. Modernist examples include William Whitfield's 1966–70 extension to the Institute of Chartered Accountants and the 1963–71 extension to Ulster Museum by Francis Pym, in which classicism is dramatically juxtaposed with brutalist mass. A similar spirit of playfulness is evident in DK-CM's interventions too, which appropriated elements from Fullwell Cross Library, a listed 1960s building by Frederick Gibberd, and in the jewellery box of muf's **Hypocaust Pavilion**, built at St Albans in 2004. Tim Ronalds's refurbishment of the listed Hackney Empire (2001–4) embellishes the gaudy colour scheme introduced in the 1970s by Mecca Bingo, while an extension bearing giant terracotta lettering complements the lively vulgarity of Frank Matcham's theatre.

Where next for post-modernism? A cautionary last word from Sam Jacob of FAT, pointing out both the pitfalls and profits of cultural inheritance:

> First: No historical jokes. Yes to projects about absence, loss, flatness, impossibility. But please, no bloody jokes for the sake of it. Yes too to pathos, rhetoric and provocation. Yes to reference but no to overblown self-reference. In other words, weed out all that historically inflected commercial schlock. Get rid of fun-for-fun's-sake. Bin the pseudo-academic references. But treasure those moments that make us break our stride, double-take and suddenly think about the nature of the world.[3]

Queen's Building

School of Engineering and Sustainable Development,
De Montfort University, Mill Lane, Leicester
1991–3, Short Ford & Associates

Alan Short was teaching part-time at Leicester Polytechnic in 1989 when he entered a competition for a new engineering building there, intended from the first to have low energy costs. The Queen's Building became the campus's flagship when it was elevated to university status in 1992.

The building uses natural sources of heat, light and ventilation. It is therefore narrow, a contrast to the deep office plans of the previous 15 years, with massive load-bearing masonry walls that provide an equable climate, while cross and stack effect ventilation removes peak temperatures. Shallow laboratories are stitched together in a rambling, twisted plan, with electrical laboratories at one end, mechanical laboratories at the other, with larger general laboratories, lecture theatres and larger teaching rooms in the middle. The top-floor drawing office is angled so the rooflights all face north, as at Stirling and Gowan's engineering building elsewhere in the city.

The notion of form following function has never been more appropriate than here, where the all-important service ducts are made the dominant features. Short had begun his career in Ted Cullinan's office with a love of the Gothic revival, and gave sources for the brick decoration that ranged from William Butterfield and Frank Furness to Norman Shaw to Hendrik Berlage. The mortar matched the brickwork, as at Lord Leighton's Kensington studio. The interior is dominated by a glazed brick atrium with a genuine 19th-century ambiance; only the built-in steel seating on its upper levels, set unnervingly over the void, is reminiscent of that at Cullinan's Uplands Conference Centre (1982–6).

Avenue de Chartres Car Park

Chichester, West Sussex
1990–1, Birds Portchmouth Russum (BPR)

Until the arrival of the railways, the Roman origins of Chichester's town plan were legible and dominant: a polygonal wall reinforced by bastions and main streets named after the cardinal points, radiating out to city gates. Successive layers of transport infrastructure to the south – railway, ring road, coach park – had weakened the sense of an edge between the walled town and its hinterland. It is not without irony that it took a multi-storey car park to engage with the situation.

What Birds Portchmouth Russum contributed in effect was a new stretch of city wall, providing a processional route to the city while at the same time screening their car park and the urban sprawl that lay behind. Colour-coded aisles provide a safe pedestrian route on the parking decks, while stair towers connect to a wall walk, also known as an allure in castle terminology, that spans the approach road before descending to the ground.

Whereas most car parks are concrete frames over which is slipped a brick tea cosy, Chichester makes a rhetorical distinction between the tailored orange-red brick of the ramparts and towers and the exposed structure of the parking decks. Originally designed in stone, the civic front was later changed to brick, incorporating diagonal patterns of honeycomb bond (for ventilation) and dark blue headers (reflecting the Sussex vernacular). As in the work of BPR's former mentor, James Stirling, there is exuberance in the details as well as the big gestures: as the pedestrian bridge-cum-portal arches over the Avenue de Chartres it is supported by their version of Trajan's Column in Rome.

Geffrye Museum Extension

Kingsland Road, Shoreditch, London
1997–8, Branson Coates, executive architects Sheppard Robson

The museum is housed in a 1712–14 almshouse, built with a bequest from Sir Robert Geffrye for the widows of City ironmongers. It was initially converted in 1912–13 by the London County Council as a museum of furniture and woodworking, intended as a resource for Shoreditch cabinetmakers. In the 1930s, curator Marjorie Quennell installed a chronological sequence of domestic interiors. Branson Coates were appointed in 1992 to design a new wing to house the museum's 20th-century collections.

The wing is located unobtrusively, at the rear. Visitors emerge from the almshouse into a light, open-plan link that has an undulating diagonal lattice roof punctuated by yellow mushroom columns. The extension takes the shape of a horseshoe or magnet, bending Quennell's chronological timeline so that visitors are taken on an arc, ending up where they began. Between the two brick gable ends of the horseshoe is the glass entrance to the new galleries and a central flying staircase that unwinds around a copper newel. The sensual and multi-layered interior reflects Nigel Coates's interest in spatial narratives.

Views out are carefully controlled and a sinuous ramp provides a route down to gardens. Slanting brickwork in Flemish bond spirals around the exterior walls, inspired by the twisted brick soffits of a skewed railway bridge. In Wright & Wright's 2016 master plan to expand the museum, the main entrance is relocated so that the Branson Coates extension will become a central reception space.

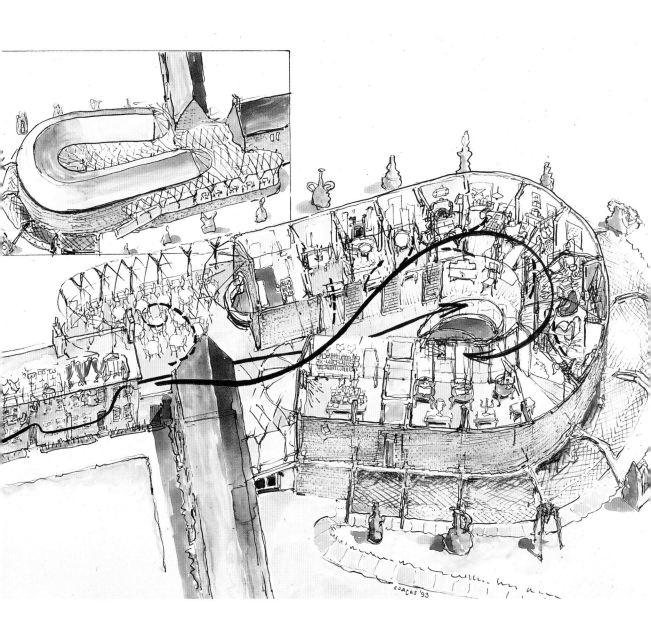

Blue House

2A-C Garner Street, Hackney, London
2000–2, FAT

More first album than manifesto, Sean Griffiths's sky-blue house packs years of accumulated thinking into a tight space. Built for £365,000 on a former metalworkers' yard, it combines the architect's family house with an office for his wife and a separate rental flat. Detailed to appear as skinny as a signboard – Griffiths originally wanted to rent out the façade as advertising space – the exterior balances formal techniques of scaling and distortion with a restrained palette of colour and materials.

Industrial products are manipulated to make an ironic commentary on vernacular or craft traditions, such as the cement-fibre clapboarding, which is stamped with a repetitive grain pattern. A cut-out dolls' house and gridded windows communicate the live/work programme, while tree silhouettes sprout from the garden wall. The tension of the compressed street front is released in the symmetrical windows, sequin panels and mannerist pediment of the long side elevation.

Contrasting with the cartoonish exterior is the intricate interior, which weaves the three domains together using spatial elements from Adolf Loos's *Raumplan* concept, the Vanna Venturi house and layered baroque planning. As at Charles Jencks's **Thematic House**, a flowing, ambiguous sense of space coexists with strongly characterized rooms. The main stair winds around the first-floor bedroom in the manner of a tower house or Loos's Müller House in Prague. In 2016 Griffiths obtained planning permission for a roof extension based on a series of overlapping shed forms.

Islington Square

New Islington, Manchester
2005–6, FAT

This mixture of two- and three-dimensional thinking recurs at Islington Square, a loop of 23 terraced houses for the Manchester Methodist Housing Association. It forms part of New Islington, a redevelopment of the 1970s Cardroom estate in Ancoats. Master-planned by Will Alsop and developed by Urban Splash with the regeneration agency English Partnerships, the 12-hectare site was one of seven Millennium Communities Programme areas launched in 1997 by the New Labour Government.

Like Ralph Erskine's Byker Estate in Newcastle, the format and appearance of Islington Square was guided by extensive consultation with future residents. Their aspirations – street-level front doors, gardens front and rear, garages, local amenities – had to be reconciled with the regeneration goals of sustainability, high densities and low budgets. The L-plan interiors combine fixed features such as first-floor Juliet balconies and window seats with flexible semi-open planning. Superscaled brick patterning and shaped gables respond to residents' notions of domesticity while sidestepping their deep-rooted preference for 'traditional' designs. The tension between individual choice and communal identity, figural fronts and stripped-down backs, recalls how residents personalized Le Corbusier's modernist housing at Pessac in the decades after it was completed.

Hypocaust Pavilion

St Albans, Hertfordshire
2003–4, muf architecture/art

In 1932, Tessa Verney Wheeler excavated Building 8 in the Roman town of Verulamium, squeezing through the tunnels of its underfloor heating system or hypocaust. She carefully unearthed its 2nd-century geometric mosaic, which was left *in situ* and protected by a utilitarian brick box. In 1999 a competition for a replacement structure was won by muf.

The resulting enigmatic white pavilion sits lightly amongst the football and picnics of Verulamium Park, approached via a retaining wall that marks the extent of Building 8. The ends of the flat roof tilt upwards, creating a glazed gap; mirrored soffits allow glimpses of the mosaic on approach. Enclosing walls of pre-cast panels of glassfibre reinforced concrete (GRC) form a lightweight superstructure that has a minimal impact on the buried archaeology. Oyster shells in the aggregate provide tactility and a link to the past – oysters being a Roman delicacy (hundreds of shells were found in the house's well) and their shells used as aggregate in Roman concrete. Rosettes of varying sizes pierce the walls, cookie-cutter style, with their shape derived from a motif within the mosaic floor. A door-sized window marks the original entrance to the mosaic room.

Sunshine Children's Centre

Civic Square, Tilbury, Essex
2007, Featherstone Young

On the strength of their South Essex Rape and Incest Crisis Centre (SERICC) of 2004–5, at nearby Grays, Thurrock Council commissioned Featherstone Young to remodel an existing children's disability centre, based at the annexe to Tilbury's neo-Georgian library. Tilbury's fortunes have been closely tied to the nearby docks, whose 1960s expansion supplanted London's Docklands. But many jobs were lost with containerization, leaving the town with a legacy of high unemployment rates and gaps in educational attainment, skills and health.

The centre offers a range of activities to children and young people with physical disabilities or special educational needs. The architects devised workshops with the children, using drawings and shadow puppetry as a starting point for a fun graphic language that was applied to the façades, signage, windows and interior.

A semi-open play space, a sensory room, and an arts, crafts and IT studio are placed on one side of the central reception, with an office and quiet counselling room on the other. The main play area is defined by curvy windows with deep, brightly coloured projections that are deep enough to clamber into. Elsewhere, tiny porthole windows stimulate curiosity about the world outside. Mezzanine storage platforms are over clad with tree-shaped cut-outs. A new entrance is highlighted by a chunky 's' for Sunshine, providing a welcoming entrance and asserting the Centre's presence within the town.

Fullwell Cross Interventions

Barkingside High Street, Redbridge, Greater London
2014, DK-CM

In 1958 Frederick Gibberd was commissioned by Ilford Council to design
a new library and swimming pool in the inter-war suburb of Barkingside.
Revisions to the brief and local government reorganization delayed
construction until 1965–8, by which time the area had been absorbed into
Greater London. The library, with its scalloped concrete dome and crisp pre-
cast panels, was listed at grade II in 2007.

Planned around an inward-facing civic square, the complex has a distant
relationship with the street. As part of a package of improvements funded by
the London Borough of Redbridge with the Greater London Authority, DK-CM
drew upon the building's details to enhance the public realm. They replicated
the arches of Gibberd's lantern, unfurling them to create a loggia against
the blank wall of the former vapour baths. The arches are drawn out at the
corners and at the end to form an entrance canopy to the leisure centre.
With its green concrete spandrels (matching the copper dome) and bold
terrazzo pavement (based on the lobby to the baths), one might mistakenly
assume that the arcade had come first.

At the other end of the leisure centre a high brick wall was removed
to create a new green space, as well as a retail unit and public convenience,
housed in a timber-clad, scaled down version of the swimming baths. DK-
CM's dialogue with Gibberd's architecture is playful, responsive and socially
engaged.

The Green

Nunhead, Southwark, London
2015–16, AOC

Nunhead Green, a sliver of open space fringed with stock brick terraces and pubs, is a typical south London relict village, overtaken by waves of Victorian and 20th-century housing. Its evolution continues with a community centre that, along with the re-landscaping of Nunhead Green proper, represents the first phase of AOC's master plan for this diverse but gentrifying area. Part-funded by an adjoining terrace of private houses also designed by AOC, the centre is run by local community group Nunhead's Voice.

The street front bustles with local references, architectural allusions and a brick materiality. It is as if half of the split pediment of the Vanna Venturi house has been pushed forward, and grown an embossed herringbone texture in sympathy with the adjacent Tudorbethan-style pub. In place of the central chimneystack in Venturi's house is a lantern. A mint green steel balcony complete with supergraphics greets the visitor, held up by a cut-out caryatid. For architects, this is a reference to Berthold Lutbetkin's Highpoint II; for locals, it represents Jenny Hill, a 19th-century music hall performer buried at Nunhead Cemetery.

The domestic intimacy of the interior is offset by expansive touches: the double-height, lantern-lit hall, Gehry-inspired red-stained plywood wainscoting and the diagonal staircase that crosses the reception area.

Notes

Origins

1. Charles Jencks, 'The Post-modern Agenda', in Jencks, ed., *The Post-Modern Reader*, London: Academy Editions, 1992, pp. 10–39; Jencks, *Architecture Today*, 2nd Edition, New York: Harry Abrams, 1988, pp. 187–90.
2. Joseph Hudnut, 'The Post-Modern House', *Architectural Record*, May 1945, vol 97(5), pp. 70–5.
3. Jill E Pearlman, *Inventing American Modernism: Joseph Hudnut, Walter Gropius and the Bauhaus Legacy at Harvard*, Charlottesville: University of Virginia Press, 2007, p. 6; Margaret A Rose, *The Post-Modern and the Post-Industrial: A Critical Analysis*, Cambridge: Cambridge University Press, 1991, p. 7; Tim Woods, *Beginning Post-modernism*, Manchester: Manchester University Press, 1999, p. 99.
4. Nikolaus Pevsner, 'Architecture in Our Time: Nikolaus Pevsner on the Anti-Pioneers', *The Listener*, 29 December 1966, vol. 76, no. 1970, pp. 953–5.
5. Robert Stern, *New Directions in American Architecture*, New York: George Braziller, 1977, pp. 134–5.
6. Charles Jencks, *Modern Movements in Architecture*, Harmondsworth: Penguin, Second Edition, 1985, p. 373.
7. C Ray Smith, *Supermannerism, New Attitudes in Post-Modern Architecture*, New York: Dutton, 1977, p. xxiii.
8. The Big Duck was constructed by Martin Maurer in 1930–1 in Riverhead, Long Island. It is now a protected building, placed on the National Register of Historic Places in 1997.
9. Paolo Portoghesi, *Post-modern: the Architecture of the Post-industrial Society*: New York, Rizzoli, 1982, p. 11.
10. 'Six British Architects', *Architectural Design*, vol. 51, no. 12, December 1981, pp. 106–11.
11. John Outram, *Architects' Lives*, C467/86, National Sound Archive, British Library, recorded 1 April 2008.
12. Charles Jencks, 'The Revisionists of Modern Architecture', in Barbara Goldstein, ed., *Architecture: Opportunities, Achievements*, London: RIBA, 1977, pp. 55–62.
13. Kenneth Frampton, 'Towards a Critical Regionalism: Six Points for an Architecture of Resistance', in Hal Foster, ed., *'Anti-Aesthetic', Essays on Post-modern Culture*, Seattle: Bay Press, 1983, pp. 16–30.
14. Nikolaus Pevsner, *North-West and South Norfolk (The Buildings of England)*, Harmondsworth: Penguin, 1962, p. 69, 45–7 (p. 46).

Houses and Housing

1. Nicholas Taylor, 'The Failure of Housing', *Architectural Review*, vol. 142, no. 849, November 1967, p. 341.
2. Nicholas Taylor, *The Village in the City*, London: Temple Smith, 1973, p. 144.
3. Will Hutton, *The State We're In, Why Britain is in Crisis and How to Overcome it*, London: Vintage (paperback edition), 1996, p. 210.

Landscapes

1. Ian Hamilton Finlay, *Unconnected Sentences on Gardening*, cited in Yves Abrioux, *Ian Hamilton Finlay: A Visual Primer*, London: Reaktion Books, 1992, p. 40.

Civic Buildings

1. Robert Venturi, Thomas Cubitt Lecture, Royal Society of Arts, 8 April 1987, published in *RSA Journal*, vol. 136, no. 5378, January 1988, pp. 89–103.
2. Edward Cullinan, 'Tradition and Nostalgia', in Kenneth Powell, *Edward Cullinan Architects*, London: Academy Editions, 1995, pp. 91–3.
3. James Stirling, 'The Katharine Stephen Room', in Ruth Rosenthal and Maggie Toy, eds., *Building*

Sights, London: Academy Editions, 1995, p. 49.

4. Adam Sharr and Stephen Thornton, *Demolishing Whitehall*, Aldershot: Ashgate, 2013, p. 254.

5. John Summerson, 'Heavenly Mansions: An Interpretation of Gothic,' in *Heavenly Mansions and other Essays on Architecture*, London: Cresset Press, 1949, p. 1.

6. *Church Building*, no. 15, Summer 1990, pp. 45-7 (p. 46).

Commercial Buildings

1. Jonathan Meades, 'Better Standard of Ordinariness', *Architects' Journal*, vol. 171, no. 1, 2 January 1980, pp. 4-6.

2. Charles Jencks, *Critical Modernism: Where is Post-Modernism Going?*, Chichester: Wiley-Academy, 2007, p. 60.

3. Rab Bennetts, 'Separating Fact from Fiction on Broadgate: An Architect's Perspective', unpublished text of May 2011, kindly supplied by Rab Bennetts.

4. Jencks, op. cit., p. 61.

5. George Orwell, 'Good Bad Books', *Tribune*, 2 November 1945, reprinted in *The Penguin Essays of George Orwell*, London: Penguin, 1994, pp. 318-21.

6. As quoted in a letter from the Twentieth Century Society to the Royal Borough of Kensington and Chelsea, 19 August 2014.

7. Mark Girouard, *Big Jim: the Life and Work of James Stirling*, London: Chatto & Windus, 1998, p. 75.

James Stirling

1. Reyner Banham, 'Stirling Escapes the Hobbits', *New Society*, vol. 70, no. 1137, 4 October 1984, pp. 15-6 (p. 15).

2. Cited in Ian Latham, 'Drawing Conclusions: Working with Stirling', *Architecture Today*, no. 217, April 2011, pp. 8-17.

3. John Jacobus, *James Stirling: Buildings & Projects, 1950-1974*, London: Thames and Hudson, 1975.

4. Geoffrey H Baker, *The Architecture of James Stirling*

and his Partners James Gowan and Michael Wilford, Farnham: Ashgate, 2011, p. 180.

5. Colin Rowe and Fred Koetter, 'Collage City', *Architectural Review*, vol. 158, no. 942, August 1975, pp. 66-91.

6. Baker, op. cit., p. 386 and 'Omnibus: James Stirling', directed by Michael Blackwood, broadcast on BBC1, 22 May 1987. Excerpt at https://www.youtube.com/watch?v=Wu2r-JEWYVg, accessed 26 February 2017

7. James Stirling, 'Lecture '81', Denys Lasdun (ed.) *Architecture in an Age of Scepticism*, New York: Oxford University Press, 1984, pp. 192-213.

8. Girouard, op. cit., p. 216.

9. Stirling interview with Michael Dennis, 'Sackler Sequence', *Architectural Review*, vol. 180, no. 1073, July 1986, pp. 26-33 (p. 30).

10. Girouard, op. cit., p. 224.

11. Thomas Muirhead, James Stirling and Michael Wilford (eds.), *James Stirling Michael Wilford and Associates: Buildings & Projects 1975-1992*, London: Thames & Hudson, 1994, p. 251.

12. Girouard, *Big Jim*, p. 284.

13. Hugh Pearman, 'Stirling's Rising Value', *The Sunday Times*, 14 April 1991.

14. Baker, op. cit., p.232.

Terry Farrell

1. Interview with Clare Melhuish in Stephen Dobney (ed.) *Terry Farrell: Selected and Current Works*, Mulgrave, Victoria, Australia: Images Publishing, 1994, p. 9.

2. Terry Farrell, *Place: A Story of Modelmaking, Menageries and Paper Rounds*, London: Laurence King, 2004, p. 145, p. 12.

3. Deyan Sudjic, 'The Man Who Took High-Tech Out to Play', *Sunday Times*, 16 January 1983, pp. 26-31 (p. 29).

4. Farrell, op. cit., p. 27.

5. Kenneth Powell, 'Terry Farrell, Jeremy Dixon and

the Beginnings of Post-Modernism in England',
The Seventies, Twentieth Century Architecture 10,
London: Twentieth Century Society, 2012, pp.
153–63 (p. 158).

6. Sudjic, op. cit., p. 26.

7. Jonathan Glancey, 'Love Me Do', *The Independent*,
13 November 1995, p. 9.

8. Farrell, op. cit., p. 12.

CZWG

1. Peter Cook, '75 New Architects', *Architectural
Design*, vol. 41, no. 12, December 1971, pp. 753–61
(p. 755).

2. 'Negozi a Londra', *Domus*, no. 480, November
1969, p. 480.

3. 'Interview: Piers Gough', *Transition*, vol. 3, no. 2,
February 1983, pp. 11–5 (p. 13).

4. Cook, op. cit., p. 755.

5. Piers Gough, personal communication, 12
December 2016.

6. Deyan Sudjic, 'Architecture's B Movie Hero',
Blueprint, no. 26, April 1986, pp. 16–9 (p. 19).

7. 'Six British Architects', *Architectural Design*, vol. 51,
no. 12, December 1981, pp. 106–8 (p.106).

8. Piers Gough, personal communication, 12
December 2016.

9. Piers Gough, 'Embracing D&B: the Seven-year
Itch', talk given at 2007 RIBA Research Symposium,
transcript at https://www.architecture.com/files/
ribaprofessionalservices/researchanddevelopment/
piersgough.pdf, accessed 26 January 2017.

10. 'Interview: Piers Gough', op. cit., pp. 11–5 (p. 13).

11. Sudjic, op. cit., p. 16.

12. *CZWG, English Extremists: The Architecture of
Campbell Zogolovitch Wilkinson Gough*, London:
Fourth Estate, 1988, p. 15.

12. 'Six British Architects', op. cit., p. 106.

14. Martin Pawley, 'The house that Janet built', *The
Guardian*, 17 October 1988.

15. Hermione Hobhouse, ed., *Survey of London:

Volumes 43 and 44, Poplar, Blackwall and Isle
of Dogs*, London: English Heritage, 1994, pp.
466–80. British History Online http://www.
british-history.ac.uk/survey-london/vols43-4/
pp466-480

John Outram

1. John Outram, interviewed in Beatriz Colomina,
Urtzi Grau, Craig Buckley, eds., *Clip, Stamp,
Fold, the Radical Architecture of Little Magazines,
196X to 197X*, New York: Actar Publishers, M+M
Books, Media and Modernity Program, Princeton
University, 2010, p. 453.

2. John Outram, 'Six British Architects', *Architectural
Design*, vol. 51, no. 12 December 1981, pp. 108.

3. *Country Life*, vol. 194, no. 38, 21 September 2000,
pp. 124–9.

Legacy

1. Charles Jencks, *The Story of Post-modernism*,
Chichester: John Wiley & Sons Ltd, 2011.

2. FAT, 'Postmodernism – An Incomplete Project',
in *Architectural Design* (issue on Radical Post-
Modernism; guest editors, Charles Jencks, Sean
Griffiths, Charles Holland and Sam Jacob), vol.
81, no. 5, September/October 2011. The phrase
inverts Jürgen Habermas (1983) 'Modernity – An
Incomplete Project,' in Foster (ed.) op. cit.,
pp. 3–15.

3. Sam Jacob, 'Post-modernism's real qualities
are mean and difficult, yet also psychedelically
positive', 13 August 2015, https://www.
dezeen.com/2015/08/13/sam-jacob-opinion-
postmodernism-revival-we-are-all-postmodern-
now/, accessed 26 February 2017.

Further Reading

Adamson, G, Pavitt, J, *Postmodernism: Style and Subversion, 1970–90*, London: V&A Publishing, 2011

Ghirardo, D, *Architecture after Modernism*, London: Thames and Hudson, 1996

Jacobs, J, *The Death and Life of Great American Cities*, New York: Random House, 1961

Jencks, C, *The Language of Post-Modern Architecture*, New York: Rizzoli, 1977, with revised editions in 1978, 1980, 1984, 1988 and 1991

Jencks, C, *Post-Modern Classicism*, London: Academy Editions, 1980

Jencks, C (ed.), 'Post-Modernism & Discontinuity', *Architectural Design*, vol. 57, no. 1/2, January/February 1987

Jencks, C, *The Story of Post-Modernism: Five Decades of the Ironic, Iconic and Critical in Architecture*, Chichester: John Wiley & Sons, 2011

Jencks, C et al (eds.), 'Radical Post-Modernism', *Architectural Design*, vol. 81, no. 5 September/October 2011

Klotz, H, *Moderne und Postmoderne: Architektur der Gegenwart*, 1984. English edition: *The History of Postmodern Architecture*, Cambridge, MA: MIT Press, 1988

Portoghesi, P, *After Modern Architecture*, New York: Rizzoli, 1982

Rossi, A, *Architettura della Città*, 1966. English edition: *The Architecture of the City*, Cambridge, MA: MIT Press, 1982

Rowe, C and Koetter, F, *Collage City*, Cambridge, MA: MIT Press, 1978

Stern, R, *Modern Classicism*, New York: Rizzoli, 1988

Szacka, L–C, Exhibiting the Postmodern: The 1980 Venice Architecture Biennale, Venice: Marsilio Editori S.p.A., 2017

Venturi, R, *Complexity and Contradiction in Architecture*, New York: Museum of Modern Art, 1966; 2nd ed. 1977

Venturi, R, Scott-Brown, D and Izenour, S, *Learning from Las Vegas: The Forgotten Symbolism of Architectural Form*, Cambridge, MA: MIT Press, 1972

Index

237

Acknowledgements

To architects Laurence Bain, Nigel Coates, Jeremy Dixon, Terry Farrell, Sarah Featherstone of Featherstone Young Architects, Liza Fior of muf architecture/art, Bruce Gilbreth, Piers Gough and Rex Wilkinson of CZWG, Charles Holland, Charles Jencks, Edward Jones, David Knight of DK-CM, John Melvin, Thomas Muirhead, John and Rima Outram, Richard Pierce, Mike Russum of Birds Portchmouth Russum Architects, Geoff Shearcroft of AOC Architecture, Alan Short.

To the following for access: Charles Jencks; Christopher and Henrietta McCall; Becky Trotman and Gerry Sullivan at Thames Water; Mark Vale at Kingswood; Jonathan Vining; Andrew Cameron at The Circle; Alex Wright at Thames Water Reading. To Lucy Millson-Watkins for additional photography.

To the following for stimulating discussion: Barnabas Calder, Charles Jencks, Adam Nathaniel Furman, Owen Hopkins of Sir John Soane's Museum, Léa-Catherine Szacka, Timothy Brittain-Catlin.

To our colleagues at Historic England, in particular Susie Barson, Veronica Fiorato, Emily Gee, Pete Herring, Deborah Mays, Posy Metz and Patience Trevor, and the photographers Steven Baker, Anna Bridson, James O Davies, Pat Payne and Chris Redgrave. Historic England is assessing a number of post-modern buildings in England for possible inclusion on the National Heritage List for England (NHLE).

To Nicola Newman and her team at Batsford.

Picture credits

First published in the United Kingdom in 2017 by
Batsford
43 Great Ormond Street
London
WC1N 3HZ

An imprint of Pavilion Books Company Ltd

ISBN 978-1-84994-450-2

A CIP catalogue record for this book is available from the British Library.

10 9 8 7 6 5 4 3 2 1

Reproduction by Mission Productions Ltd, Hong Kong
Printed and bound by Toppan Leefung, China

This book can be ordered direct from the publisher at www.pavilionbooks.com

The text face is Mendoza, designed by José Mendoza y Almeida and released in 1991.
The titles are set in Ano Stencil, designed by Gareth Hague in 2015.